Project Management
Complete Self-Assessment Guide

CW00540898

The guidance in this Self-Assessment is base
best practices and standards in business pro
and quality management. The guidance is al
judgment of the individual collaborators listed in the Acknowledgments.

Notice of rights

Trademarks

Table of Contents

About The Art of Service

The Art of Service, Business Process Architects since 2000, is dedicated to helping stakeholders achieve excellence.

Defining, designing, creating, and implementing a process to solve a stakeholders challenge or meet an objective is the most valuable role… In EVERY group, company, organization and department.

Unless you're talking a one-time, single-use project, there should be a process. Whether that process is managed and implemented by humans, AI, or a combination of the two, it needs to be designed by someone with a complex enough perspective to ask the right questions.

Someone capable of asking the right questions and step back and say, 'What are we really trying to accomplish here? And is there a different way to look at it?'

With The Art of Service's Standard Requirements Self-Assessments, we empower people who can do just that — whether their title is marketer, entrepreneur, manager, salesperson, consultant, Business Process Manager, executive assistant, IT Manager, CIO etc... —they are the people who rule the future. They are people who watch the process as it happens, and ask the right questions to make the process work better.

Contact us when you need any support with this Self-Assessment and any help with templates, blue-prints and examples of standard documents you might need:

http://theartofservice.com
service@theartofservice.com

Acknowledgments

This checklist was developed under the auspices of The Art of Service, chaired by Gerardus Blokdyk.

Representatives from several client companies participated in the preparation of this Self-Assessment.

In addition, we are thankful for the design and printing services provided.

Included Resources - how to access

Included with your purchase of the book is the Project Management Self-Assessment Spreadsheet Dashboard which contains all questions and Self-Assessment areas and auto-generates insights, graphs, and project RACI planning - all with examples to get you started right away.

How? Simply send an email to
access@theartofservice.com
with this books' title in the subject to get the Project Management Self Assessment Tool right away.

You will receive the following contents with New and Updated specific criteria:

- The latest quick edition of the book in PDF

- The latest complete edition of the book in PDF, which criteria correspond to the criteria in...

- The Self-Assessment Excel Dashboard, and...

- Example pre-filled Self-Assessment Excel Dashboard to get familiar with results generation

- In-depth specific Checklists covering the topic

- Project management checklists and templates to assist with implementation

INCLUDES LIFETIME SELF ASSESSMENT UPDATES

Every self assessment comes with Lifetime Updates and Lifetime Free Updated Books. Lifetime Updates is an industry-first feature which allows you to receive verified self assessment updates, ensuring you always have the most accurate information at your fingertips.

Get it now- you will be glad you did - do it now, before you forget.

Send an email to **access@theartofservice.com** with this books' title in the subject to get the Project Management Self Assessment Tool right away.

Your feedback is invaluable to us

If you recently bought this book, we would love to hear from you! You can do this by writing a review on amazon (or the online store where you purchased this book) about your last purchase! As part of our continual service improvement process, we love to hear real client experiences and feedback.

How does it work?
To post a review on Amazon, just log in to your account and click on the Create Your Own Review button (under Customer Reviews) of the relevant product page. You can find examples of product reviews in Amazon. If you purchased from another online store, simply follow their procedures.

What happens when I submit my review?
Once you have submitted your review, send us an email at review@theartofservice.com with the link to your review so we can properly thank you for your feedback.

Purpose of this Self-Assessment

This Self-Assessment has been developed to improve understanding of the requirements and elements of Project Management, based on best practices and standards in business process architecture, design and quality management.

It is designed to allow for a rapid Self-Assessment to determine how closely existing management practices and procedures correspond to the elements of the Self-Assessment.

The criteria of requirements and elements of Project Management have been rephrased in the format of a Self-Assessment questionnaire, with a seven-criterion scoring system, as explained in this document.

In this format, even with limited background knowledge of Project

Management, a manager can quickly review existing operations to determine how they measure up to the standards. This in turn can serve as the starting point of a 'gap analysis' to identify management tools or system elements that might usefully be implemented in the organization to help improve overall performance.

How to use the Self-Assessment

On the following pages are a series of questions to identify to what extent your Project Management initiative is complete in comparison to the requirements set in standards.

To facilitate answering the questions, there is a space in front of each question to enter a score on a scale of '1' to '5'.

1 Strongly Disagree

2 Disagree

3 Neutral

4 Agree

5 Strongly Agree

Read the question and rate it with the following in front of mind:

'In my belief, the answer to this question is clearly defined'.

There are two ways in which you can choose to interpret this statement;
1. how aware are you that the answer to the question is clearly defined
2. for more in-depth analysis you can choose to gather

evidence and confirm the answer to the question. This obviously will take more time, most Self-Assessment users opt for the first way to interpret the question and dig deeper later on based on the outcome of the overall Self-Assessment.

A score of '1' would mean that the answer is not clear at all, where a '5' would mean the answer is crystal clear and defined. Leave emtpy when the question is not applicable or you don't want to answer it, you can skip it without affecting your score. Write your score in the space provided.

After you have responded to all the appropriate statements in each section, compute your average score for that section, using the formula provided, and round to the nearest tenth. Then transfer to the corresponding spoke in the Project Management Scorecard on the second next page of the Self-Assessment.

Your completed Project Management Scorecard will give you a clear presentation of which Project Management areas need attention.

Project Management Scorecard Example

Example of how the finalized Scorecard can look like:

Project Management Scorecard

Your Scores:

BEGINNING OF THE
SELF-ASSESSMENT:

CRITERION #1: RECOGNIZE

INTENT: Be aware of the need for change. Recognize that there is an unfavorable variation, problem or symptom.

In my belief, the answer to this question is clearly defined:

5 Strongly Agree

4 Agree

3 Neutral

2 Disagree

1 Strongly Disagree

1. What problems are you facing and how do you consider Project Management will circumvent those obstacles?
<--- Score

2. What requirements do you need to know before you acquire PaaS?
<--- Score

3. What problems have you come across or are you facing?
<--- Score

4. What do you need to do to accomplish the goal or goals?
<--- Score

5. Is project management knowledge necessary for a successful event?
<--- Score

6. What would happen if Project Management weren't done?
<--- Score

7. What should trigger a replacement or rehabilitation of an asset?
<--- Score

8. Who else hopes to benefit from it?
<--- Score

9. Troubleshooting – are problems related to what is actually changing (the change), to the management of tasks and resources to make the change happen (project management) or to issues relating to employee engagement, buy-in and resistance (Change Management)?
<--- Score

10. Should you invest in industry-recognized qualifications?
<--- Score

11. What are two common project management

practices that prevent an organization from meeting its goals?

<--- Score

12. To what extent would your organization benefit from being recognized as a award recipient?

<--- Score

13. How do you deal with problems that arise when you are working in groups?

<--- Score

14. What are two common project management practices that prevent your organization from meeting its goals?

<--- Score

15. Who is needed to fulfill this project?

<--- Score

16. There is lots of discussion about the role of a project manager; whether a project manager is needed in the agile world or not. How much and which way a traditional project manager has to change his/her management style or way of working in order to be an agile project manager?

<--- Score

17. What does the PMO need to do to provide support to your organization?

<--- Score

18. Can management personnel recognize the monetary benefit of Project Management?

<--- Score

19. Why do you need Portfolio Management?
<--- Score

20. Who would oversee the project – do you need a Project Steering Group, or will this be done by the Executive Team?
<--- Score

21. Does Project Management create potential expectations in other areas that need to be recognized and considered?
<--- Score

22. Are the required resources available or need to be acquired?
<--- Score

23. Are there any unresolved technical issues, organization coordination, or information confirmations that need to be resolved prior to kickoff?
<--- Score

24. How much project management is needed?
<--- Score

25. What will prevent the Manager/Director/ Head of the PMO from gaining a disproportionate amount of control?
<--- Score

26. Are there recognized Project Management problems?
<--- Score

27. Is the need for organizational change recognized?
<--- Score

28. What are the stakeholder objectives to be achieved with Project Management?
<--- Score

29. To what extent does management recognize Project Management as a tool to increase the results?
<--- Score

30. What business goals and user needs will be addressed?
<--- Score

31. What are the minority interests and what amount of minority interests can be recognized?
<--- Score

32. Have you involved the people who really know what the system needs to deliver?
<--- Score

33. How much accuracy is needed?
<--- Score

34. When is it needed?
<--- Score

35. What threats might prevent us from getting there?
<--- Score

36. Are controls defined to recognize and contain

problems?
<--- Score

37. Procurement management, when is this needed?
<--- Score

38. Have all staff that need training in Privacy policy and procedures been identified?
<--- Score

39. As a sponsor, customer or management, how important is it to meet goals, objectives?
<--- Score

40. To what extent does each concerned units management team recognize Project Management as an effective investment?
<--- Score

41. Does your organization need a PMO?
<--- Score

42. What needs to be accomplished?
<--- Score

43. What was the main reason or need for establishing PMO in yourr oganization?
<--- Score

44. What does Project Management success mean to the stakeholders?
<--- Score

45. Who needs to receive a copy of the Meeting Minutes?

<--- Score

46. Identify: is the critical path the constraint?
<--- Score

47. How do you justify the need for a project, the request for investment by your investors?
<--- Score

48. How are you going to measure success?
<--- Score

49. How are the Project Management's objectives aligned to the group's overall stakeholder strategy?
<--- Score

50. Needs project management?
<--- Score

51. What practices helps your organization to develop its capacity to recognize patterns?
<--- Score

52. Are there project dependencies and sequencing issues (such as schedule, architecture, resources, requirements, etc.) needing coordination?
<--- Score

53. Will the metrics and measurement techniques to determine project success (or failure) need to change?
<--- Score

54. How do you meet the users needs?
<--- Score

55. At what efficiency do you need to run to bring the schedule back on track?
<--- Score

56. How much are sponsors, customers, partners, stakeholders involved in Project Management? In other words, what are the risks, if Project Management does not deliver successfully?
<--- Score

57. What threats might prevent you from getting there?
<--- Score

58. What does your team need?
<--- Score

59. What are your business needs?
<--- Score

60. Will a response program recognize when a crisis occurs and provide some level of response?
<--- Score

61. What are the customer needs that indicate PaaS may be appropriate?
<--- Score

62. Outside the project team, how many people need to be kept up to date on the project progress?
<--- Score

63. Are Project Management changes recognized early enough to be approved through the regular

process?
<--- Score

64. Are there any specific expectations or concerns about the Project Management team, Project Management itself?
<--- Score

65. Do you really need software?
<--- Score

66. Why is the problem important?
<--- Score

67. Why do you need a PMO?
<--- Score

68. How do you identify the constraint?
<--- Score

69. Who is going to deliver the service offerings that have been identified?
<--- Score

70. Is the existing status accounting sufficient and appropriate for the projects needs?
<--- Score

71. Issues of feasibility; can you do the project?
<--- Score

72. Why is a communication event taking place?
<--- Score

73. What are the expected benefits of Project Management to the stakeholder?

<--- Score

74. What are the skills needed to be successful in an agile environment?
<--- Score

75. What are the users needs?
<--- Score

76. Have you identified the critical path for the project?
<--- Score

77. How do you stay flexible and focused to recognize larger Project Management results?
<--- Score

78. Do you really need a PMO?
<--- Score

79. When a Project Management manager recognizes a problem, what options are available?
<--- Score

80. What situation(s) led to this Project Management Self Assessment?
<--- Score

81. When a vendor discloses open source, what do they need to tell you?
<--- Score

82. Are employees recognized or rewarded for performance that demonstrates the highest levels of integrity?
<--- Score

83. What specialized emergency information is needed by people with various disabilities in an emergency?
<--- Score

84. What skills do you need to iterate?
<--- Score

85. What resources do you need for each task?
<--- Score

Add up total points for this section:
_____ = Total points for this section

Divided by: _____ (number of
statements answered) = _____
Average score for this section

Transfer your score to the Project
Management Index at the beginning of
the Self-Assessment.

CRITERION #2: DEFINE:

INTENT: Formulate the stakeholder problem. Define the problem, needs and objectives.

In my belief, the answer to this question is clearly defined:

5 Strongly Agree

4 Agree

3 Neutral

2 Disagree

1 Strongly Disagree

1. How do you define throughput and how does your organization benefit from maximizing it?
<--- Score

2. Has everyone on the team, including the team leaders, been properly trained?
<--- Score

3. Are there contextual conditions, such as the size

of the project or nature of the task, that signal a better fit for agile versus traditional project management approaches?
<--- Score

4. Is there a completed, verified, and validated high-level 'as is' (not 'should be' or 'could be') stakeholder process map?
<--- Score

5. What are the compelling stakeholder reasons for embarking on Project Management?
<--- Score

6. Have the customer needs been translated into specific, measurable requirements? How?
<--- Score

7. When is/was the Project Management start date?
<--- Score

8. What would be the goal or target for a Project Management's improvement team?
<--- Score

9. What are the dynamics of the communication plan?
<--- Score

10. Has anyone else (internal or external to the group) attempted to solve this problem or a similar one before? If so, what knowledge can be leveraged from these previous efforts?
<--- Score

11. When are adjustments required?
<--- Score

12. How will the Project Management team and the group measure complete success of Project Management?
<--- Score

13. Are you using the ERP system to fulfill other project management requirements?
<--- Score

14. Does implementation of project management require a culture change?
<--- Score

15. Has the direction changed at all during the course of Project Management? If so, when did it change and why?
<--- Score

16. Have current policies and procedures been compared to HIPAA Privacy requirements?
<--- Score

17. Is the Project Management scope manageable?
<--- Score

18. Is the current 'as is' process being followed? If not, what are the discrepancies?
<--- Score

19. What is the required timing for completion?
<--- Score

20. How do you determine how much time a task requires?
<--- Score

21. What infrastructure is required to deliver working software every week?
<--- Score

22. Are stakeholder processes mapped?
<--- Score

23. Does each requirement contribute to a specific project objective?
<--- Score

24. Who are the Project Management improvement team members, including Management Leads and Coaches?
<--- Score

25. What are the requirements for this procurement?
<--- Score

26. Is data collected and displayed to better understand customer(s) critical needs and requirements.
<--- Score

27. Are team charters developed?
<--- Score

28. Project management: are there sufficient numbers of procurement and program staff with required knowledge and skills to implement and administer the contracts?
<--- Score

29. How is the team tracking and documenting its

work?
<--- Score

30. Precisely what are the detailed Business Requirements?
<--- Score

31. Are there any constraints known that bear on the ability to perform Project Management work? How is the team addressing them?
<--- Score

32. How well defined are the acceptance criteria for project deliverables?
<--- Score

33. Is there a completed SIPOC representation, describing the Suppliers, Inputs, Process, Outputs, and Customers?
<--- Score

34. What is the business case of this project?
<--- Score

35. What about when your context is not so simple?
<--- Score

36. How was the 'as is' process map developed, reviewed, verified and validated?
<--- Score

37. What customer feedback methods were used to solicit their input?
<--- Score

38. How did the Project Management manager receive input to the development of a Project Management improvement plan and the estimated completion dates/times of each activity?
<--- Score

39. If you require your organization to have Agile experience, are you artificially limiting the vendor pool?
<--- Score

40. Is the team formed and are team leaders (Coaches and Management Leads) assigned?
<--- Score

41. Is Project Management linked to key stakeholder goals and objectives?
<--- Score

42. What critical content must be communicated – who, what, when, where, and how?
<--- Score

43. Does the team have regular meetings?
<--- Score

44. Has the project scope been baselined?
<--- Score

45. Is the team adequately staffed with the desired cross-functionality? If not, what additional resources are available to the team?
<--- Score

46. Is the project in response to situations that require sensitivity and neutrality?

<--- Score

47. Is there regularly 100% attendance at the team meetings? If not, have appointed substitutes attended to preserve cross-functionality and full representation?
<--- Score

48. How do you capture requirements?
<--- Score

49. Has/have the customer(s) been identified?
<--- Score

50. What constraints exist that might impact the team?
<--- Score

51. Are the project objectives clearly defined?
<--- Score

52. What is the meaning of success in this context?
<--- Score

53. What are the Roles and Responsibilities for each team member and its leadership? Where is this documented?
<--- Score

54. When are meeting minutes sent out? Who is on the distribution list?
<--- Score

55. Is Project Management currently on schedule according to the plan?
<--- Score

56. How often are the team meetings?
<--- Score

57. How does the Project Management manager ensure against scope creep?
<--- Score

58. How is agile project management performed in the context of virtual teams?
<--- Score

59. What is the scope of the law organizations services?
<--- Score

60. Do the problem and goal statements meet the SMART criteria (specific, measurable, attainable, relevant, and time-bound)?
<--- Score

61. Will an interface be required to accounting, HR, timekeeping, purchasing or project management software?
<--- Score

62. Has the Project Management work been fairly and/or equitably divided and delegated among team members who are qualified and capable to perform the work? Has everyone contributed?
<--- Score

63. What are the rough order estimates on cost savings/opportunities that Project Management brings?
<--- Score

64. Has a project plan, Gantt chart, or similar been developed/completed?
<--- Score

65. When it comes to requirements management for projects and programs, how are high-performing organizations doing better or differently than low performers?
<--- Score

66. Has the improvement team collected the 'voice of the customer' (obtained feedback – qualitative and quantitative)?
<--- Score

67. Which is constrained (typically scope, time and,or quality)?
<--- Score

68. Are improvement team members fully trained on Project Management?
<--- Score

69. Is full participation by members in regularly held team meetings guaranteed?
<--- Score

70. What type of import and export facilities do you require?
<--- Score

71. Is there a Project Management management charter, including stakeholder case, problem and goal statements, scope, milestones, roles and responsibilities, communication plan?

<--- Score

72. How do you keep key subject matter experts in the loop?
<--- Score

73. What are the boundaries of the scope? What is in bounds and what is not? What is the start point? What is the stop point?
<--- Score

74. Has a high-level 'as is' process map been completed, verified and validated?
<--- Score

75. Is a proof of concept required to demonstrate capability?
<--- Score

76. Are customer(s) identified and segmented according to their different needs and requirements?
<--- Score

77. How will variation in the actual durations of each activity be dealt with to ensure that the expected Project Management results are met?
<--- Score

78. Are different versions of process maps needed to account for the different types of inputs?
<--- Score

79. Is the team sponsored by a champion or stakeholder leader?
<--- Score

80. Are customers identified and high impact areas defined?
<--- Score

81. Is there a critical path to deliver Project Management results?
<--- Score

82. What specifically is the problem? Where does it occur? When does it occur? What is its extent?
<--- Score

83. When is the estimated completion date?
<--- Score

84. Do you have a good case?
<--- Score

85. Is a fully trained team formed, supported, and committed to work on the Project Management improvements?
<--- Score

86. Has a team charter been developed and communicated?
<--- Score

87. What key stakeholder process output measure(s) does Project Management leverage and how?
<--- Score

88. Are there different segments of customers?
<--- Score

89. Do you meet the experience requirement?
<--- Score

90. Will team members perform Project Management work when assigned and in a timely fashion?
<--- Score

91. Business case - what value would delivering the project bring to your organization?
<--- Score

92. Will team members regularly document their Project Management work?
<--- Score

93. Is the team equipped with available and reliable resources?
<--- Score

94. If substitutes have been appointed, have they been briefed on the Project Management goals and received regular communications as to the progress to date?
<--- Score

95. What aspects are required for deploying CCPM in your organization?
<--- Score

96. Is the improvement team aware of the different versions of a process: what they think it is vs. what it actually is vs. what it should be vs. what it could be?
<--- Score

Add up total points for this section:
_ _ _ _ _ = Total points for this section

Divided by: _ _ _ _ _ _ (number of

statements answered) = _____
Average score for this section

Transfer your score to the Project
Management Index at the beginning of
the Self-Assessment.

CRITERION #3: MEASURE:

INTENT: Gather the correct data. Measure the current performance and evolution of the situation.

In my belief, the answer to this question is clearly defined:

5 Strongly Agree

4 Agree

3 Neutral

2 Disagree

1 Strongly Disagree

1. How much will this project cost?
<--- Score

2. What key measures identified indicate the performance of the stakeholder process?
<--- Score

3. Do you need all UML diagrams in a project?
<--- Score

4. What is the cost variance (CV=EV-AC)?
<--- Score

5. How will jettisoning certain processes and structure impact the business?
<--- Score

6. The functions of the project management and the business analysis in an agile environment: do you need both?
<--- Score

7. Do you have simple, objective measures of Project health status ?
<--- Score

8. How will you measure the projects progress?
<--- Score

9. Does your organization focus on improving processes with legal project management principles/tools?
<--- Score

10. What are the metrics and measures of successful legal project management?
<--- Score

11. What has the team done to assure the stability and accuracy of the measurement process?
<--- Score

12. What impact does predictability have on project management throughout your organization?

<--- Score

13. What data was collected (past, present, future/ongoing)?
<--- Score

14. How does the Design Thinking approach to project management differ from the Rational Analytic approach?
<--- Score

15. How do you minimize impact and cost?
<--- Score

16. Did the implementation of PMO have measurable impacts in terms of project success?
<--- Score

17. What are the key input variables? What are the key process variables? What are the key output variables?
<--- Score

18. What might increase costs beyond the budget?
<--- Score

19. Who are the key individuals or organizations that you should focus on?
<--- Score

20. What charts has the team used to display the components of variation in the process?
<--- Score

21. Which element can vary (based on priority)?
<--- Score

22. Are there any organization programs focussing on public procurement?

<--- Score

23. Is there a Performance Baseline?

<--- Score

24. What should be included in your project charter contents?

<--- Score

25. How does your organization with multiple projects prioritize them?

<--- Score

26. What are ways that organizational culture impacts project management, and how do you manage the already stated?

<--- Score

27. How will the ventures bottom line be impacted over the next year if you do not do this project now?

<--- Score

28. Do you embark on the journey to become more customer focused, to speed up your delivery process, to align your organization, and to ensure more quality?

<--- Score

29. What is the impact to the end user?

<--- Score

30. Is there an effective project management process, with cost and timing goals, for new

product start-ups?
<--- Score

31. Scope, cost, quality, time, available resources - which are most fixed?
<--- Score

32. Are key measures identified and agreed upon?
<--- Score

33. What particular quality tools did the team find helpful in establishing measurements?
<--- Score

34. Cost goals: how much should it cost?
<--- Score

35. What is common and special cause variation in project management?
<--- Score

36. How do you prioritize the cost, schedule, quality and scope to determine what's critical?
<--- Score

37. What events could occur that may adversely impact upon the objective of the procurement?
<--- Score

38. What is the cost of the project management solution?
<--- Score

39. Did you conduct an alternatives analysis for each project?
<--- Score

40. What is the impact of the agile movement on the future of project management?

<--- Score

41. What are your organizations priorities for onboarding practice connection projects?

<--- Score

42. Who participated in the data collection for measurements?

<--- Score

43. Was a life-cycle cost analysis performed?

<--- Score

44. Is a solid data collection plan established that includes measurement systems analysis?

<--- Score

45. Rather than scope, cost, and schedule, exploration projects should be measured on vision, cost, and schedule. Did the project deliver a valuable product (implemented vision) to the customer?

<--- Score

46. Did you conduct an alternatives analysis for this project?

<--- Score

47. What does the project charter include?

<--- Score

48. What is the sequence of UML diagrams in your project?

<--- Score

49. How are you assessing the environment calls for an investigation into the projects impact to know if it will it be very high profile or low key?
<--- Score

50. What Cost Control Tool Do Many Experts Say is Crucial to Project Management?
<--- Score

51. Who might be involved in developing a charter?
<--- Score

52. Whats the current status of the project in terms of scope, time, cost, quality and risk?
<--- Score

53. To what extent are problems caused by human decisions and practices?
<--- Score

54. Who will be impacted by this procurement?
<--- Score

55. Assessing the environment calls for an investigation into a projects impact do you know if a project will be very high profile or low key?
<--- Score

56. What are the key factors, conditions, assumptions and potential risks that impact the estimate?
<--- Score

57. Are high impact defects defined and identified in the stakeholder process?
<--- Score

58. How do you measure current performance?
<--- Score

59. What are the agreed upon definitions of the high impact areas, defect(s), unit(s), and opportunities that will figure into the process capability metrics?
<--- Score

60. What are the costs of procurement and who bears them?
<--- Score

61. What could cause delays in the schedule?
<--- Score

62. What is the purpose of your top priority project?
<--- Score

63. How does your communication impact or change the project?
<--- Score

64. Are process variation components displayed/ communicated using suitable charts, graphs, plots?
<--- Score

65. How does cost of change affect software?
<--- Score

66. Do you account for Cost-Benefit Analysis with examples?

<--- Score

67. Cost goals: What should it cost?
<--- Score

68. What is the efficiency of current inventory management systems, including warehousing and distribution costs?
<--- Score

69. Scenario analysis is used as a Requirements investigation technique?
<--- Score

70. What are the impacts and consequences of the procurement?
<--- Score

71. What is the impact if you do not do it now?
<--- Score

72. Who constitutes the PMO team (key roles, org chart)?
<--- Score

73. What is the current status of the project in terms of scope, time, cost, quality and risk?
<--- Score

74. How do you measure customer value and project managements contribution to that value?
<--- Score

75. Is Process Variation Displayed/Communicated?
<--- Score

76. Is data collected on key measures that were identified?

<--- Score

77. Have you developed a milestone chart or produced a gantt chart?

<--- Score

78. What core services will the PMO provide, and how will success/value be measured?

<--- Score

79. Have you found any 'ground fruit' or 'low-hanging fruit' for immediate remedies to the gap in performance?

<--- Score

80. How much will it cost?

<--- Score

81. Is data collection planned and executed?

<--- Score

82. What Does the PMO Charter Define?

<--- Score

83. Was a data collection plan established?

<--- Score

84. Is key measure data collection planned and executed, process variation displayed and communicated and performance baselined?

<--- Score

85. How do you prepare your cost estimates?

<--- Score

86. How will the existing culture and organizational structure be impacted by agile project management?

<--- Score

87. What will the entire project cost?

<--- Score

88. How large is the gap between current performance and the customer-specified (goal) performance?

<--- Score

89. How sure are you about the conditions that could impact the outcome of this particular project?

<--- Score

90. Is long term and short term variability accounted for?

<--- Score

Add up total points for this section:
_ _ _ _ _ = Total points for this section

Divided by: _ _ _ _ _ _ (number of statements answered) = _ _ _ _ _ _
Average score for this section

Transfer your score to the Project Management Index at the beginning of the Self-Assessment.

CRITERION #4: ANALYZE:

INTENT: Analyze causes, assumptions and hypotheses.

In my belief, the answer to this question is clearly defined:

5 Strongly Agree

4 Agree

3 Neutral

2 Disagree

1 Strongly Disagree

1. Is there documentation of the decision-making process available?
<--- Score

2. How does your organization know whether its project management processes are effective?
<--- Score

3. What is the organization and processes of your project management (conditions, contracts,

implementation, service, etc.)?
<--- Score

4. What is the cost of poor quality as supported by the team's analysis?
<--- Score

5. Are pertinent alerts monitored, analyzed and distributed to appropriate personnel?
<--- Score

6. What were the crucial 'moments of truth' on the process map?
<--- Score

7. What quality tools were used to get through the analyze phase?
<--- Score

8. Which stakeholder characteristics are analyzed?
<--- Score

9. What conclusions were drawn from the team's data collection and analysis? How did the team reach these conclusions?
<--- Score

10. Review the current state of your software development process – is it chaotic, or does it have some order and structure that you generally follow?
<--- Score

11. Have the problem and goal statements been updated to reflect the additional knowledge gained from the analyze phase?

<--- Score

12. What are the current procurement processes/ workflows, and strengths and weaknesses?
<--- Score

13. Is data and process analysis, root cause analysis and quantifying the gap/opportunity in place?
<--- Score

14. What is your change control process?
<--- Score

15. How effective was the project management processes, and what could be improved?
<--- Score

16. What part of the procurement process are you in?
<--- Score

17. Did any value-added analysis or 'lean thinking' take place to identify some of the gaps shown on the 'as is' process map?
<--- Score

18. Do you have sufficient understanding of how the data maintained by the system is used?
<--- Score

19. What are the four processes that are essential for a strategic project management office to be successful?
<--- Score

20. Are there any special risks associated with

maintaining the integrity of the data?
<--- Score

21. Have the concerns of stakeholders to help identify and define potential barriers been obtained and analyzed?
<--- Score

22. How do you ensure that the already stated selected projects are given the best opportunity to succeed from the very start?
<--- Score

23. How do you identify and analyze stakeholders and their interests?
<--- Score

24. What are the processes and infrastructure?
<--- Score

25. How does the concept of statistical process control apply to tasks?
<--- Score

26. What are the requirements for data and metadata management?
<--- Score

27. Does the project management office / portfolio management process help reinforce enterprise architecture?
<--- Score

28. Was a cause-and-effect diagram used to explore the different types of causes (or sources of variation)?
<--- Score

29. Does Project Management systematically track and analyze outcomes for accountability and quality improvement?
<--- Score

30. Have the types of risks that may impact Project Management been identified and analyzed?
<--- Score

31. What does the data say about the performance of the stakeholder process?
<--- Score

32. How do you ensure that knowledge and experience of management processes are available among people in various positions leading the project?
<--- Score

33. Are gaps between current performance and the goal performance identified?
<--- Score

34. What tools were used to narrow the list of possible causes?
<--- Score

35. What types of data must be collected and entered into the system?
<--- Score

36. Do staff have the necessary skills to collect, analyze, and report data?
<--- Score

37. Did any additional data need to be collected?
<--- Score

38. Is the performance gap determined?
<--- Score

39. Who are the primary participants in the integration process?
<--- Score

40. Have changes been properly/adequately analyzed for effect?
<--- Score

41. What were the financial benefits resulting from any 'ground fruit or low-hanging fruit' (quick fixes)?
<--- Score

42. Is there an approval process for policies and procedures?
<--- Score

43. What tools were used to generate the list of possible causes?
<--- Score

44. How has your organization created a process for selection that obtains the best software for the best price and at the same time obtain organizational Buy-In?
<--- Score

45. What are your organizations most important external opportunities and threats?
<--- Score

46. Where is there great opportunity for Procurement to increase its contribution?
<--- Score

47. Is the gap/opportunity displayed and communicated in financial terms?
<--- Score

48. What are the (financial, other) risks associated with the procurement process?
<--- Score

49. Do you want to transform your skills, data, and business?
<--- Score

50. Is there a process to correct deficiencies found as a result of inadequate staff training?
<--- Score

51. Was a detailed process map created to amplify critical steps of the 'as is' stakeholder process?
<--- Score

52. Is the project team identified and qualified?
<--- Score

53. What could you do differently to improve the product or process?
<--- Score

54. Were Pareto charts (or similar) used to portray the 'heavy hitters' (or key sources of variation)?
<--- Score

55. During which procurement processes does

procurement negotiation occur?

<--- Score

56. Do organizational routines or traditions affect the development of the procurement process?

<--- Score

57. Do you find this process to procure products and services adequate?

<--- Score

58. What are customers expectations of the process?

<--- Score

59. Does your organization have a formal process in place to implement organizational change?

<--- Score

60. Does your organization systematically track and analyze outcomes related for accountability and quality improvement?

<--- Score

61. What project management (PM) process is least understood?

<--- Score

62. Do you understand the development process well enough to be able to identify and evaluate the key risks?

<--- Score

63. How would you assess the maturity of the Portfolio Management Process Documentation process area?

<--- Score

64. What specific process modifications or additions are required for rapid ROI?
<--- Score

65. What are the revised rough estimates of the financial savings/opportunity for Project Management improvements?
<--- Score

66. How well does the Portfolio Management Process Documentation process area work?
<--- Score

67. Processes supporting this project?
<--- Score

68. Who will assist with importing users, facility/asset data, and historical data into the system?
<--- Score

69. What are the procedures for improvement of current processes?
<--- Score

70. What kind and quality of outputs and by when will they be produced?
<--- Score

71. What sort of data do you input in the system?
<--- Score

72. Problem-solving: based on the data, can your organization identify what it needs to do?
<--- Score

73. Regarding data access for contractors. Should they be granted the same legal access to records and other data as counterparts?
<--- Score

74. What is the consequence of the process of procurement push along the supply chain for meeting client expectation and delivering added value?
<--- Score

75. What are the principles of data protection and security that are in place?
<--- Score

76. Are there communication processes in place?
<--- Score

77. What customer-visible objects are produced as output?
<--- Score

78. Have any additional benefits been identified that will result from closing all or most of the gaps?
<--- Score

79. Are all lightweight and agile project management process steps applicable to your organization?
<--- Score

80. Have all non-recommended alternatives been analyzed in sufficient detail?
<--- Score

81. Can agility work with a waterfall project management process in your setting?
<--- Score

82. What project management qualifications does the Project Manager have?
<--- Score

83. What resources go in to get desired output after changes?
<--- Score

84. What would you change in your overall process?
<--- Score

85. Were any designed experiments used to generate additional insight into the data analysis?
<--- Score

86. Has your organization implemented any process of continuous improvement?
<--- Score

87. How do you reduce the size of the data set to be more relevant and workable?
<--- Score

88. Are losses documented, analyzed, and remedial processes developed to prevent future losses?
<--- Score

89. Does your organization have a formal Risk Management process in place to assess and mitigate risks to the organization?

<--- Score

90. What did the team gain from developing a sub-process map?
<--- Score

91. Will there be a Change Control Process in place?

<--- Score

92. Is the Project Management process severely broken such that a re-design is necessary?
<--- Score

93. What are your key Project Management indicators that you will measure, analyze and track?

<--- Score

94. What data types are required?

<--- Score

95. Does the project management office / portfolio management process work closely with enterprise architecture?

<--- Score

96. Were there any improvement opportunities identified from the process analysis?
<--- Score

97. Which existing processes, tools and templates for executing projects can be applied to the agile project management framework?

<--- Score

98. Who is expected to participate in the development process and how often?
<--- Score

99. What function does the software perform to transform input data into output?
<--- Score

100. How was the detailed process map generated, verified, and validated?
<--- Score

101. How do you balance increased investment in the requirements process with the need to be agile?
<--- Score

Add up total points for this section:
_ _ _ _ _ = Total points for this section

Divided by: _ _ _ _ _ _ (number of
statements answered) = _ _ _ _ _ _
Average score for this section

Transfer your score to the Project
Management Index at the beginning of
the Self-Assessment.

CRITERION #5: IMPROVE:

INTENT: Develop a practical solution. Innovate, establish and test the solution and to measure the results.

In my belief, the answer to this question is clearly defined:

5 Strongly Agree

4 Agree

3 Neutral

2 Disagree

1 Strongly Disagree

1. How do you improve your project management, estimating, scheduling, budgeting, testing, etc., through the use of this information?
<--- Score

2. The fundamentals of agile software development, agile project management, and evolutionary development have been proven and demonstrated to be highly successful. Are these

now preferred in our organization?
<--- Score

3. Are improved process ('should be') maps modified based on pilot data and analysis?
<--- Score

4. Does application of project management practices ultimately create a better product or provide no real value to the Agile development life cycle?
<--- Score

5. Is there a high level of maturity and experience with agile-scrum project management, solution development and delivery?
<--- Score

6. What information or documents will you need for your project application work?
<--- Score

7. Is agile project management applicable in the context of product development?
<--- Score

8. Is pilot data collected and analyzed?
<--- Score

9. What communication items need improvement?
<--- Score

10. How can users act as knowledge co-producers in the design and development stages?
<--- Score

11. How does the solution remove the key sources of issues discovered in the analyze phase?
<--- Score

12. Are attitudes of your organizations staff regarding project work improving?
<--- Score

13. Is the meaning of each requirement easily understood and easy to read?
<--- Score

14. What are your best practices that improve project management of distributed software development?
<--- Score

15. How can the technical work of dozens, or even hundreds, of developers be coordinated without the usual project management apparatus?
<--- Score

16. Governance, which encompasses all of the decision making and project management for an application, begins with business case development. Does it really make sense to build this application?
<--- Score

17. Is there a cost/benefit analysis of optimal solution(s)?
<--- Score

18. What are the credentials of the team members and do they understand your issues?
<--- Score

19. What is the best online project management solution website projects integrating Google Apps?
<--- Score

20. How could a new product or service be developed in this century without Agile Project Management?
<--- Score

21. What challenges do the various cloud solutions present?
<--- Score

22. What triggers a decision to go forward with a capital project?
<--- Score

23. Have all system acceptance test results been reviewed and accepted?
<--- Score

24. How are risks managed for the project?
<--- Score

25. Evaluate your ideas about project management - do they support or undermine risk management?
<--- Score

26. What tools were used to tap into the creativity and encourage 'outside the box' thinking?
<--- Score

27. Are attitudes of the organizations staff

regarding project work improving?
<--- Score

28. To what extent are project decisions made with stakeholder benefits in mind?
<--- Score

29. What is the chance of which risk occurring?
<--- Score

30. What error proofing will be done to address some of the discrepancies observed in the 'as is' process?
<--- Score

31. Is source code freely available to all developers, at the same time?
<--- Score

32. Do you already have documents that can form the basis of document automation tools?
<--- Score

33. Are new and improved process ('should be') maps developed?
<--- Score

34. What are the most important benefits for us of effective organizational risk management?
<--- Score

35. What business results do you expect to achieve when you are successful?
<--- Score

36. Can agile project management be adopted by industries other than software development?

<--- Score

37. How can distributed software development be agile?
<--- Score

38. What is Project Management's impact on utilizing the best solution(s)?
<--- Score

39. What tools were used to evaluate the potential solutions?
<--- Score

40. What attendant changes will need to be made to ensure that the solution is successful?
<--- Score

41. In-house software development: what project management practices lead to success?
<--- Score

42. What is the strategy for managing the risks?
<--- Score

43. What were the underlying assumptions on the cost-benefit analysis?
<--- Score

44. Do not agile methods address the challenges of 21st century systems (i.e., high-risk, time-sensitive, R&D-oriented, new product and service development projects)?
<--- Score

45. Is the optimal solution selected based on testing

and analysis?
<--- Score

46. Is the intent and purpose of the document identified?
<--- Score

47. Is the level of budget contingency in line with the project risks?
<--- Score

48. Are policies and procedures for security of the crime scene understood by all parties?
<--- Score

49. How will the team or the process owner(s) monitor the implementation plan to see that it is working as intended?
<--- Score

50. Is there a small-scale pilot for proposed improvement(s)? What conclusions were drawn from the outcomes of a pilot?
<--- Score

51. Originally, agile project management required collocated teams. How can a new product or service be developed without them?
<--- Score

52. Is the implementation plan designed?
<--- Score

53. How do you evaluate project management performance?
<--- Score

54. How are the risks in a project finance transaction allocated?
<--- Score

55. If the PMO will face the necessity of facilitating organization-wide change, with whom will they collaborate (e.g. with your organization Development Officer)?
<--- Score

56. What are the challenges in project management of distributed software development?
<--- Score

57. Has the project development environment been established?
<--- Score

58. How well did the Project Team understand the expectations of specific roles and responsibilities?
<--- Score

59. How does the software to be built fit into a larger system, product, or business context and what constraints are imposed as a result of the context?
<--- Score

60. Was a pilot designed for the proposed solution(s)?
<--- Score

61. If outside of your sphere of responsibility, how can you influence the decision-makers?
<--- Score

62. What are the business requirements that drive PaaS decisions?

<--- Score

63. Who were involved in the decision making of establishing the PMO?

<--- Score

64. What risks should be included in the Key Risk Register?

<--- Score

65. How much has your financial/project management staffing changed as a result of ERP workload changes?

<--- Score

66. What areas need improvement?

<--- Score

67. What is in it for the executives to support an improved project management practice?

<--- Score

68. In what area do you think PMO plays a major role in improving project performance?

<--- Score

69. In our organization is it perfectly legitimate for a pm to ask, can you explain why the task will take that long, and the risk of shortening it?

<--- Score

70. What is the risk of people or resources not being available when needed?

<--- Score

71. For each major risk, what are some approaches you can use?
<--- Score

72. What is the implementation plan?
<--- Score

73. Who is currently involved in purchasing operations and decision-making and what are responsibilities?
<--- Score

74. Who takes decisions on managing projects?
<--- Score

75. What are the tools used to support project management of distributed software development?
<--- Score

76. Is a solution implementation plan established, including schedule/work breakdown structure, resources, risk management plan, cost/budget, and control plan?
<--- Score

77. What do you think might be typical areas that project face risks?
<--- Score

78. How do you conduct procurement of equipment e.g. Bidders conference, proposal evaluation etc ?
<--- Score

79. The location of the solution?
<--- Score

80. Evaluate the information requirements for other systems. Will an interface be required to accounting, HR, timekeeping, purchasing or project management software?
<--- Score

81. How and why does CCPM contribute to improved project management in practice?
<--- Score

82. Are the best solutions selected?
<--- Score

83. What should the role of project management be with respect to the deliverables of your development projects?
<--- Score

84. What communications are necessary to support the implementation of the solution?
<--- Score

85. Who has the greater degree of control over the risk eventuality?
<--- Score

86. What does the 'should be' process map/design look like?
<--- Score

87. What lessons, if any, from a pilot were incorporated into the design of the full-scale solution?

<--- Score

88. How will the group know that the solution worked?
<--- Score

89. How did the team generate the list of possible solutions?
<--- Score

90. What is the primary function of the Activity Decomposition Decision Tree?
<--- Score

91. Do employees, employees and organization staff understand what to do in the event of a violent incident?
<--- Score

92. Is there a required training program for all newly appointed development managers designed to familiarize them with software project management?
<--- Score

93. Has a procurement strategy been developed?
<--- Score

94. Is the project manager a risk?
<--- Score

95. How effective was the documentation that you received with the project product/service?
<--- Score

96. Do you know whether the underpinning

contracts support short development timelines and undefined deliverables?

<--- Score

97. How can the benefits of PM training programs be improved?

<--- Score

98. Are possible solutions generated and tested?

<--- Score

99. Describe the design of the pilot and what tests were conducted, if any?

<--- Score

100. What are the key risks facing the project?

<--- Score

101. Do you document disagreements and work towards resolutions?

<--- Score

102. What do we mean by risk mitigation?

<--- Score

103. Are the project stakeholders comfortable with the results of the project?

<--- Score

104. What is your agile risk management and when does it make sense to use it?

<--- Score

105. How effective is your organization in detecting and evaluating risks in its external environment?

<--- Score

106. How could the WBS help you develop a realistic budget?

<--- Score

107. To what extent was the evolution of risks communicated?

<--- Score

108. What of the risk of rework if initial architecture work overlooks what turns out to be critical? what is the probability of this happening?

<--- Score

109. What is the team's contingency plan for potential problems occurring in implementation?

<--- Score

110. Is the coordination with subcontractors documented?

<--- Score

111. Developed the business case?

<--- Score

112. To what degree will you be able to track usage to assess any benefits of document automation?

<--- Score

113. Were any criteria developed to assist the team in testing and evaluating potential solutions?

<--- Score

114. What tools were most useful during the improve phase?

<--- Score

115. What is the current software project management and development environment?
<--- Score

116. Are there any constraints (technical, political, cultural, or otherwise) that would inhibit certain solutions?
<--- Score

117. Is a contingency plan established?
<--- Score

118. Does the software Quality Assurance function have a management reporting channel separate from the software development project management?
<--- Score

119. Why should a client choose a project team which offers agile software development?
<--- Score

Add up total points for this section:
_____ = Total points for this section

Divided by: _____ (number of statements answered) = _____
Average score for this section

Transfer your score to the Project Management Index at the beginning of the Self-Assessment.

CRITERION #6: CONTROL:

INTENT: Implement the practical solution. Maintain the performance and correct possible complications.

In my belief, the answer to this question is clearly defined:

5 Strongly Agree

4 Agree

3 Neutral

2 Disagree

1 Strongly Disagree

1. What type of training requirements and learning curve were involved in adopting the product?
<--- Score

2. Who can benefit from corresponding standards of protection?
<--- Score

3. Does the response plan contain a definite closed

loop continual improvement scheme (e.g., plan-do-check-act)?

<--- Score

4. Does job training on the documented procedures need to be part of the process team's education and training?

<--- Score

5. Has planning started for a start up workshop (or series of workshops)?

<--- Score

6. Why should your organization spend all of this effort on planning when there is so much work to be done?

<--- Score

7. What are the controls of CCPM in your organization?

<--- Score

8. Is new knowledge gained imbedded in the response plan?

<--- Score

9. Has the improved process and its steps been standardized?

<--- Score

10. Is knowledge gained on process shared and institutionalized?

<--- Score

11. Is a response plan in place for when the input, process, or output measures indicate an 'out-of-

control' condition?
<--- Score

12. What key inputs and outputs are being measured on an ongoing basis?
<--- Score

13. If the project no longer needs a detailed master project plan, why does it need a project manager?
<--- Score

14. Do project teams perceive the Lessons Learned process is adding value?
<--- Score

15. What tools and controls are used?
<--- Score

16. Does the project plan identify a change management plan, or where it is located?
<--- Score

17. Is there a documented and implemented monitoring plan?
<--- Score

18. How long do you allow in the plan for a task ?
<--- Score

19. What is the recommended frequency of auditing?
<--- Score

20. What controls were diminished / rejected ?
<--- Score

21. What are the critical parameters to watch?
<--- Score

22. What controls have been diminished/ introduced (since CCPM) ?
<--- Score

23. Project Management Plan /Schedule — Is there an integrated Project Schedule?
<--- Score

24. Is there a transfer of ownership and knowledge to process owner and process team tasked with the responsibilities.
<--- Score

25. What standards will be used to evaluate the quality of the deliverables?
<--- Score

26. How will the process owner and team be able to hold the gains?
<--- Score

27. Are the procurement policies, procedures, manuals and/or standard contract documentation up to date, easy to use and understood by staff?
<--- Score

28. What were the lessons learned?
<--- Score

29. Does the project plan identify a communication plan, or where it is located?
<--- Score

30. That is fine as far as it goes, and does this scale?
<--- Score

31. Does the project plan identify an issue management and escalation plan, or where it is located?
<--- Score

32. Does the data migration plan identify the scope of the data migration?
<--- Score

33. Are there processes and tools to support maintaining project plans and schedules?
<--- Score

34. Have project management standards and procedures been identified / established and documented?
<--- Score

35. If standardized procurement documents are needed, where can they be found?
<--- Score

36. Have you carried out a stakeholder analysis and planned accordingly?
<--- Score

37. What should the next improvement project be that is related to Project Management?
<--- Score

38. In what ways does your organization support your efforts to learn from project work and/or share lessons learned with your team and others?

<--- Score

39. How do you merge agile, lightweight processes with standard industrial processes without either killing agility or undermining the years youve spent defining and refining your systems and software process assets?
<--- Score

40. Is there a plan to validate the effectiveness of staff training?
<--- Score

41. Is there documentation that will support the successful operation of the improvement?
<--- Score

42. How might the group capture best practices and lessons learned so as to leverage improvements?
<--- Score

43. Who is responsible for integrating the PIA outcomes back into the project plan and updating any project management paperwork?
<--- Score

44. Is reporting being used or needed?
<--- Score

45. What scenarios in terms of projected cost, schedule, and scope could/should you plan for?
<--- Score

46. What other areas of the group might benefit from the Project Management team's improvements, knowledge, and learning?

<--- Score

47. Does your communication plan identify the project communication process?
<--- Score

48. Is the project in line with the strategic plan?
<--- Score

49. What are the processes or procedures you might have in place to transfer the lessons learned to another team?
<--- Score

50. Are there implications for the observed success of agile to date that reflects on your larger understanding of organizations and fundamental nature?
<--- Score

51. Is a response plan established and deployed?
<--- Score

52. Is the Project Plan currently in use?
<--- Score

53. What quality tools were useful in the control phase?
<--- Score

54. Does the risk management plan identify the risk identification process?
<--- Score

55. Do agile projects scale with agile project management?

<--- Score

56. Does a troubleshooting guide exist or is it needed?
<--- Score

57. What is a Lessons Learned Session?
<--- Score

58. What about planning, architecture and requirements phases?
<--- Score

59. Have the risks been retired that were included in the planning stage?
<--- Score

60. How can the Lessons Learned process be improved?
<--- Score

61. Different organizational cultures affect planning?
<--- Score

62. Is a standardized process in place to track project cost information?
<--- Score

63. How will new or emerging customer needs/ requirements be checked/communicated to orient the process toward meeting the new specifications and continually reducing variation?
<--- Score

64. Do you think the PMO plays a major role in providing project teams the learned experiences

from past similar projects, before new one starts?
<--- Score

65. Our project management standards - do they support or undermine Risk Management?
<--- Score

66. Does the change management plan identify the change review and approval process?
<--- Score

67. Are suggested corrective/restorative actions indicated on the response plan for known causes to problems that might surface?
<--- Score

68. Does the test plan indicate how performance testing will be performed?
<--- Score

69. Is there a standardized process?
<--- Score

70. How often will you update the project plan?
<--- Score

71. Does the PMO play a major role in providing project teams the learned experiences from past similar projects, before a new one starts?
<--- Score

72. Are operating procedures consistent?
<--- Score

73. How will report readings be checked to effectively monitor performance?

<--- Score

74. What tools and techniques are used in planning and tracking the project?
<--- Score

75. Does the communication plan identify sample report templates?
<--- Score

76. Is there a recommended audit plan for routine surveillance inspections of Project Management's gains?
<--- Score

77. Are there documented procedures?
<--- Score

78. How will the process owner verify improvement in present and future sigma levels, process capabilities?
<--- Score

79. Is there a plan and dedicated resources to investigate and respond to audit findings?
<--- Score

80. What is the control/monitoring plan?
<--- Score

81. Does the Project Management performance meet the customer's requirements?
<--- Score

82. Do you have existing templates of procurement plans or evaluation plans for you to adapt, or will you be required to develop your own

procurement plan and evaluation plan?
<--- Score

83. Is there a control plan in place for sustaining improvements (short and long-term)?
<--- Score

84. Post project review has been planned?
<--- Score

85. Are there process theory explanations for differentiating better from less successful ways to implement agile techniques?
<--- Score

86. How will input, process, and output variables be checked to detect for sub-optimal conditions?
<--- Score

87. What if the standards of protection are breached?
<--- Score

88. Are new process steps, standards, and documentation ingrained into normal operations?
<--- Score

89. Marketing, planning and production impact the usage of project management techniques in R&D?
<--- Score

90. Has a procurement conduct plan been developed, if not, why not?
<--- Score

91. Will any special training be provided for results interpretation?
<--- Score

92. Have new or revised work instructions resulted?
<--- Score

93. What are your staff doing that other organizations can learn from?
<--- Score

94. How will the day-to-day responsibilities for monitoring and continual improvement be transferred from the improvement team to the process owner?
<--- Score

95. What role will the PMO play in Resource Planning?
<--- Score

96. Have some of the risks been retired that were included in the planning stage?
<--- Score

97. Assess the adequacy of maintenance project management standards, methodologies, and practices. Does your organization have adequate maintenance standards and controls?
<--- Score

98. If you were given the authority, what would you do in your organization to make it easier to learn from project work and share lessons learned with your team and others?
<--- Score

99. Is quality management and control performed in your organization?
<--- Score

100. Are documented procedures clear and easy to follow for the operators?
<--- Score

101. Who is the Project Management process owner?
<--- Score

102. For elder populations – how integrated and comprehensive are your stakeholders emergency plans (your continuums stakeholders)?
<--- Score

103. How long should you allow in the plan for a task ?
<--- Score

104. Is there a written quality control plan for this project?
<--- Score

105. What are the typical controls you are using now (since CCPM)?
<--- Score

106. Does the change management plan identify emergency change procedures?
<--- Score

107. In what way do you get the PMO to systematically transfer the lesson learned to others and vice versa?

<--- Score

108. Are there metrics and standards that can be used for control of agile project progress during execution?
<--- Score

109. What other systems, operations, processes, and infrastructures (hiring practices, staffing, training, incentives/rewards, metrics/dashboards/scorecards, etc.) need updates, additions, changes, or deletions in order to facilitate knowledge transfer and improvements?
<--- Score

110. Are there procurement policies, procedures, manuals and/or standard contract documentation and do they reflect a strategic approach to procurement?
<--- Score

111. Does the requirements management plan identify how changes will be identified?
<--- Score

112. Is there a Quality Assurance Plan documented and filed?
<--- Score

113. Does the project plan identify a risk management plan, or where it is located?
<--- Score

Add up total points for this section:
_ _ _ _ _ = Total points for this section

Divided by: _____ (number of
statements answered) = _____
Average score for this section

Transfer your score to the Project
Management Index at the beginning of
the Self-Assessment.

CRITERION #7: SUSTAIN:

INTENT: Retain the benefits.

In my belief, the answer to this question is clearly defined:

5 Strongly Agree

4 Agree

3 Neutral

2 Disagree

1 Strongly Disagree

1. In what respect does CCPM lead to change?
<--- Score

2. What actions will be taken if the project complexity and risk assessment rating of the preferred option exceeds existing organizational project management capacity?
<--- Score

3. If someone suggests a change to another project management practice, how can you

quickly determine if it is worth evaluating?

<--- Score

4. Who determines what tasks are included in the work breakdown structure?

<--- Score

5. What resistance to CCPM do you observe without being expressed by staff?

<--- Score

6. What resistance, related to CCPM, does staff show/express ?

<--- Score

7. Is legal project management an art, a science or a combination of both?

<--- Score

8. Project risk management is an integral component of ongoing project management. Project Managers sometimes ask, when is the best time to conduct a CRA or CEVP workshop?

<--- Score

9. What is the protocol for interaction, decision making, project management?

<--- Score

10. What are the types of projects that are being considered for the Project Management Office (PMO)?

<--- Score

11. Why should you expect the PMO to do any better?

<--- Score

12. In what way is project management software being used today?
<--- Score

13. What is the intended future state?
<--- Score

14. What is it your team members do not like about CCPM ?
<--- Score

15. What are the major differences between the Critical Chain Scheduling (CCPS) and the Traditional Project Scheduling (TPS) for your organization?
<--- Score

16. Who are the stakeholders and teams directly affected by a new product/service and are they aware?
<--- Score

17. On average, how many IT and project management professionals support your legal department?
<--- Score

18. How does critical chain help your project management ?
<--- Score

19. Do you propose the project for financing?
<--- Score

20. Why should you consider using Critical Chain Project Management?

<--- Score

21. What impact does predictability have on project management throughout an organization?

<--- Score

22. What possibilities are there to implement Agile project management in the design phase of your projects?

<--- Score

23. What is considered project work?

<--- Score

24. Is the level of detail and presentation style the same throughout?

<--- Score

25. Have you considered your project with your organization Treasurer?

<--- Score

26. Are resources not overloaded or spread thin?

<--- Score

27. Who Does Project Management?

<--- Score

28. What are the specific benefits you hope to obtain?

<--- Score

29. In what ways do you seek to empower your clients?

<--- Score

30. When does it have to be done?
<--- Score

31. How often do you take action to correct the accuracy of financial/project management information?
<--- Score

32. Who will maintain the project once it is constructed?
<--- Score

33. How can agile project management be used together with traditional project management?
<--- Score

34. How important are which benefits to your clients and your organization?
<--- Score

35. Timing: when do the effects of the communication take place?
<--- Score

36. Do PMs and the PMOs staff meet in a regular basis, throughout the project lifecycle or is it occasionally?
<--- Score

37. Who must verify corresponding reports; who can access reports; and what are the legal consequences of failing to report or misrepresentation?
<--- Score

38. What are you using for integrated CRM and Project Management Solutions?
<--- Score

39. Is a software project management tool available?
<--- Score

40. Are you investing in the right things?
<--- Score

41. Is your organization a good candidate for distributed order management?
<--- Score

42. Is the project critical to the mission or function of your organization?
<--- Score

43. Do all projects need project management?
<--- Score

44. What is the right delivery methodology to deploy?
<--- Score

45. What were the barriers you or your team faced in this situation?
<--- Score

46. What procurement procedure (open, restricted, negotiated) is used?
<--- Score

47. Who is involved in the project?

<--- Score

48. Do you utilize any project management framework for the supervision of (IT) projects?
<--- Score

49. What are the benefits and challenges of PMO?
<--- Score

50. What is the calculated Schedule Performance Index (SPI= EV/PV)?
<--- Score

51. Is this investment included in your organizations EA Transition Strategy?
<--- Score

52. Does lean & agile project management help coping with project complexity?
<--- Score

53. What is the role of project management in translating strategy from the enterprise level to the project level?
<--- Score

54. Where do you find supplementary funding?
<--- Score

55. What is your sustainable procurement?
<--- Score

56. How did CCPM change/affect your organization ?
<--- Score

57. Who will author or sign the communication?
<--- Score

58. How well does CCPM contribute to your organizations performances?
<--- Score

59. Did the project team answer questions knowledgably?
<--- Score

60. What do you hope to achieve?
<--- Score

61. What is the major challenge for the PMO in terms of knowledge transfer and project performance?
<--- Score

62. Do you have the capabilities?
<--- Score

63. What strengths do you have?
<--- Score

64. What is the project management office, and how can it help you address the unique project management challenges in your organization?
<--- Score

65. Has agile project management crossed the chasm (i.e., what is its adoption rate)?
<--- Score

66. Are your current project management and time and expense capture applications outdated

and expensive to update and maintain?
<--- Score

67. How does the structure of work affect outcomes in relation to complex systems, network theory and human dynamics?
<--- Score

68. If this measurement effort is primarily driven by project managers, what are the relationship(s) to the project management process(es)?
<--- Score

69. What are the management challenges in this effort?
<--- Score

70. Does this apply to the director of project management as well?
<--- Score

71. What business units are affected?
<--- Score

72. What will a successful outcome be?
<--- Score

73. What are the consequences for project management?
<--- Score

74. Which Project Management Knowledge Area is Least Mature?
<--- Score

75. Key problem solving knowledge resides with

the knowledge workers, and not the manager. So, how do you adapt project management techniques to deal with this key reality?
<--- Score

76. How many days work until the Project is completed ?
<--- Score

77. How is your organizations contract strategy related to project and project management activities?
<--- Score

78. Is there good contact and cooperation among procurement stakeholders?
<--- Score

79. Is the current level of personnel back-up adequate to ensure proper completion of the project?
<--- Score

80. What value would delivering the project bring to your organization?
<--- Score

81. Do you know what you are trying to achieve?
<--- Score

82. What is the reason for this project ?
<--- Score

83. Does your organization have project management methods and processes?
<--- Score

84. How do your project management competencies relate to strategy?

<--- Score

85. Is an agile-managed project more likely to succeed that one that relies on traditional approaches?

<--- Score

86. What are the key success factors?

<--- Score

87. What is agile project management?

<--- Score

88. Are the project management activities included in the WBS?

<--- Score

89. How do you know when you are finished?

<--- Score

90. What is the maturity level of the project management community?

<--- Score

91. Is there any integration with PPM for resource hours and project management?

<--- Score

92. How is organizational and national culture relevant to making project procurement choices?

<--- Score

93. Is procurement management information

maintained and easily accessible?

<--- Score

94. Is the project management office a component of the portfolio management office?

<--- Score

95. Is the coordination with subcontractors appropriate and sufficient?

<--- Score

96. Why should you change how you practice?

<--- Score

97. What activities does software project management cover?

<--- Score

98. Do you have a specialist internal procurement unit, or rely on consultants?

<--- Score

99. Does your organization have a pro bono committee?

<--- Score

100. Would you have an internal Project Manager?

<--- Score

101. What kind of features can customers expect to see in the near future?

<--- Score

102. How does the project manager use agile project management in the design stage?

<--- Score

103. What is your agile sprint backlog?
<--- Score

104. What are the limits of this approach?
<--- Score

105. Are there detailed tasks without a successor?
<--- Score

106. What people skills will your team use to help you reach consensus?
<--- Score

107. Are the project management activities included in the Project Schedule?
<--- Score

108. What part of your organization has the lead responsibility for the software?
<--- Score

109. Project management as a strategic asset: what does it look like and how do you get there?
<--- Score

110. Does the organization have a written policy on project management and an associated organizational structure?
<--- Score

111. How would you characterize the project management maturity of your organization?
<--- Score

112. Decision support system, or new practices to

improve current project management?
<--- Score

113. Are you doing what you have set out to do?
<--- Score

114. Where are the projects on schedule, performance, objectives and goals?
<--- Score

115. How do critical path projects leverage the concepts of the critical path method in your organization?
<--- Score

116. To what degree do you expect adoption of the tools, and what is the projected rate of adoption?
<--- Score

117. What is the frequency of updates?
<--- Score

118. Does your organization have a Project Management Office?
<--- Score

119. What does staff like about CCPM ?
<--- Score

120. What is the purpose of the Procurement Strategy?
<--- Score

121. Project management: how can you better design or manage this project?
<--- Score

122. What is the security track record of the software?
<--- Score

123. Does the qa function have an appropriate level of independence from project management?
<--- Score

124. What is sensitive on the project?
<--- Score

125. Are you able to demonstrate value?
<--- Score

126. Where are you in the Project Life Cycle?
<--- Score

127. Mixed agile/ traditional project management methodology, is this a reality in your organization?
<--- Score

128. In this context of Project Management, what do you do about Scrum alignment with CMMI?
<--- Score

129. What administrative authority should oversee the program?
<--- Score

130. Where does the scrum master fit in agile project manager roles and responsibilities?
<--- Score

131. Security: is the system security architecture considered?

<--- Score

132. As the project team grows in size so will the effort that has to go into management, coordination and communication?
<--- Score

133. Does your organization have the equipment and assets to do the job (computers, software and related tools)?
<--- Score

134. Could agile approaches be applied autonomously of the phases in specific projects, which normally utilise a traditional project management?
<--- Score

135. How is project scheduling done?
<--- Score

136. What will the project not deliver?
<--- Score

137. What is the level of your organizations project management maturity?
<--- Score

138. What is the rationale (logic) for using a certain type of procurement procedure?
<--- Score

139. How well do you link corporate and procurement objectives?
<--- Score

140. What are the problems/challenges in your organizations agile project management, how are decisions made?

<--- Score

141. Do you experience staff resistance related to CCPM ?

<--- Score

142. Is the management team in agreement with the purpose of the project?

<--- Score

143. What will be the success criteria?

<--- Score

144. Does ERP increase your project management efficiency?

<--- Score

145. Why, if there is a tendency to overestimate activity durations and add safety to a project, do so many projects come in behind schedule?

<--- Score

146. Why do you use phases?

<--- Score

147. How was the transformation accomplished?

<--- Score

148. Ongoing maintenance: How will your organization provide for ongoing operations and maintenance of the system?

<--- Score

149. What is the advantage of implementing CMMI in your organization?

<--- Score

150. What Projects Are Subject to our ogranizations Approval and Oversight Authority?

<--- Score

151. Why do agile projects fail?

<--- Score

152. What does the future look like?

<--- Score

153. Agile integration – at iteration retrospectives meetings the team is asked: what went well?

<--- Score

154. Are stakeholder communications adequate and effective?

<--- Score

155. Is agile right for your project?

<--- Score

156. Does your organization have the right person managing projects?

<--- Score

157. But, how do you get started?

<--- Score

158. How will services be managed and delivered?

<--- Score

159. Why do you need new project management

software?

<--- Score

160. Are there project management practices that remain constant across traditional, hybrid, and agile approaches (e.g., Risk Management, stakeholder management, team building)?

<--- Score

161. Would there be any unintended consequences of tightening targets and expanding the current procurement frameworks, such as reduced quality?

<--- Score

162. Who Uses Project Management Software?

<--- Score

163. Are employees and employees knowledgeable about what to do in an emergency?

<--- Score

164. How is perception in different areas ?

<--- Score

165. What is the project management process?

<--- Score

166. Do you know what software you are responsible for delivering?

<--- Score

167. Who are the stakeholders?

<--- Score

168. Is your organization making money at that price?

<--- Score

169. Are any companies precluded from bidding on this procurement?

<--- Score

170. When should Extreme Programming be Used?

<--- Score

171. Does scrum fulfill the project management requirements of CMMI maturity levels two to five?

<--- Score

172. Are you spending the right amount of money for specific tasks?

<--- Score

173. What is the level of compliance with the SLA?

<--- Score

174. Do the project and operation characteristics overlap?

<--- Score

175. How strong is the project management?

<--- Score

176. Does it replace or negate traditional project management concerns with risk, scheduling, metrics, and execution, or does it shift how we think about these and necessitate new techniques and approaches?

<--- Score

177. Is modularization right for your project?
<--- Score

178. Who is specifying project products/ deliverables?
<--- Score

179. From your organizational perspective, what are the trade-offs involved in shifting all project management to an agile approach, versus maintaining a mixed portfolio of agile and traditional development?
<--- Score

180. Does the project team have a similar deliverable to reuse and/or reference?
<--- Score

181. How do you select the right agile project management tool for different projects?
<--- Score

182. How do we create a culture that supports project management?
<--- Score

183. Do your Agile teams always ask Is what we are doing adding value to the product we are delivering?
<--- Score

184. Why is it important to reduce deliverables to a smallest component?
<--- Score

185. How do you rate the user interface of the

software?

<--- Score

186. How will the findings be shared internally or externally?

<--- Score

187. How do project workers perceive working in a CCPM environment ?

<--- Score

188. Can the project management team take on its own?

<--- Score

189. Availability of current and future year funding?

<--- Score

190. What are the key considerations and decisions that must be made to ensure your project management office is appropriate for your organization?

<--- Score

191. Does the supply market have a proven sustainable procurement capability?

<--- Score

192. Does your organization have a Project Management Office (PMO)?

<--- Score

193. What project management software (if any) should you use?

<--- Score

194. Which procurement types does your organization get involved in most?

<--- Score

195. Is it working?

<--- Score

196. What is the Project Management Lifecycle?

<--- Score

197. How does ccpm best practice relate to wider operations theory?

<--- Score

198. Does the system have QR coding capabilities for assets and inventory?

<--- Score

199. How will the project status be communicated during the course of the project?

<--- Score

200. What is the simplest thing that can move the project forward?

<--- Score

201. Do you use performance based procurement?

<--- Score

202. How does your agile project manager balance team level autonomy and individual level autonomy in agile software teams?

<--- Score

203. Is the project a system integration project?

<--- Score

204. What kind of people do you pick to lead agile projects?
<--- Score

205. Which will be better for project management smartsheet or asana?
<--- Score

206. Has a formal risk management program been initiated and integrated with project management?
<--- Score

207. What do you want the team to report on?
<--- Score

208. How vulnerable are you to uncertainties faced in a project?
<--- Score

209. How long will this project take?
<--- Score

210. How do you characterize the project management maturity of your organization?
<--- Score

211. Why should you estimate the project?
<--- Score

212. Do you have competent and available project management team members?
<--- Score

213. Six sigma where does it fit in project management?

<--- Score

214. Has project management and supply chain management been integrated?

<--- Score

215. Are your current project management and time and expense capture applications up to date and easy to maintain?

<--- Score

216. Have project management standards and procedures been established and documented?

<--- Score

217. Are there any principles of procurement as they relate to innovation?

<--- Score

218. Why does this matter?

<--- Score

219. What goes into your collaborative sourcing projects?

<--- Score

220. When does the project start?

<--- Score

221. How often do you use the software in a day?

<--- Score

222. How do project management and business analysis overlap?

<--- Score

223. Is the CV% or SV% greater than +/- 10%?
<--- Score

224. How is it Done?
<--- Score

225. What information does the product provide?
<--- Score

226. How can you convince your customers to use agile project management?
<--- Score

227. How will shared assets be handled for inspections, repair, and funding?
<--- Score

228. What are your organizations major strengths and weaknesses?
<--- Score

229. Are you achieving your desired objectives?
<--- Score

230. How do you obtain approval?
<--- Score

231. How are the metrics going?
<--- Score

232. Are there any drawbacks to using a responsibility assignment matrix?
<--- Score

233. How does knowledge management influence innovation and competitiveness?
<--- Score

234. How much communication is enough?
<--- Score

235. How will the project be delivered?
<--- Score

236. How will you coordinate your role responsibilities with the project supervisors role and responsibilities?
<--- Score

237. What is the business value of agile project management for creating new products and services?
<--- Score

238. Whose program is it?
<--- Score

239. What features will be implemented?
<--- Score

240. What is the role of collaborative Virtual Tools Project Management?
<--- Score

241. How do you get involved in a project with other people?
<--- Score

242. What are the essential components of corporate strategy and how are they related to the

PMO?
<--- Score

243. Do you have a formal technical architecture and strategy?
<--- Score

244. What are the communication chains?
<--- Score

245. What benefits are expected?
<--- Score

246. What is your organizational set-up of public procurement?
<--- Score

247. What are you hoping to achieve with your project communications?
<--- Score

248. How do your team members perceive CCPM ?
<--- Score

249. Are the project objectives clear and feasible?
<--- Score

250. Do you ask, what will have to be completed to accomplish this objective?
<--- Score

251. On what organization level does resistance to CCPM exist ?
<--- Score

252. What if critical path were practiced using the

best practices inherent in critical chain, such as passing on early finishes?

<--- Score

253. Are the majority of team members new to the tools used on the project?

<--- Score

254. What is happening during the Procurement Phase?

<--- Score

255. How do ITIL and agile project management coexist?

<--- Score

256. Does the project have a Quality Culture ?

<--- Score

257. What are your steps to stakeholder management and what should be accomplished in each step?

<--- Score

258. Which procurement procedure do you apply?

<--- Score

259. What is it staff does not like about CCPM ?

<--- Score

260. Is verbal or nonverbal communication more effective?

<--- Score

261. What did the introduction of CCPM mean to your projects ?

<--- Score

262. Human resources: have adequate human resources been allocated to deliver the procurement?
<--- Score

263. What resources do you already have?
<--- Score

264. Why did you start to use this management support system?
<--- Score

265. How is the role of a Project Management Office (PMO) different in an agile environment?
<--- Score

266. What are the best practices that improve project management of distributed software development?
<--- Score

267. Why are project management models not used in maintenance?
<--- Score

268. Why is it useful?
<--- Score

269. What is your compliance strategy?
<--- Score

270. How many of your staff belong to gender groups?
<--- Score

271. From whence does the money to fund a project originate?
<--- Score

272. Will you be able to make the deadline?
<--- Score

273. Has the project team delivered this deliverable on a previous project?
<--- Score

274. What are the best practices for the implementation of project management success factors?
<--- Score

275. What are significant procurements?
<--- Score

276. How do you select the right agile project management tool for different maturity levels?
<--- Score

277. Just what is a project management office, and how can it help you address the unique project management challenges in your organization?
<--- Score

278. How effective was the training you received in preparation for the use of the product/service?
<--- Score

279. Do all of the components of the project management methodology that are used work?
<--- Score

280. Do you use a Project Management Office team after concluding the transaction to ensure its success?
<--- Score

281. What is the level of your satisfaction with the project management structures, processes, and personnel?
<--- Score

282. What is the size of the incumbent workforce?
<--- Score

283. Who are the main customers for the project?
<--- Score

284. Does CCPM oppose staffs intuition of working?
<--- Score

285. Is the project an enhancement to an existing system?
<--- Score

286. What is the PMOs fundamental purpose and goals?
<--- Score

287. How often will software failures occur during operation of the system?
<--- Score

288. Product – what are you trying to accomplish and how will you know when you are finished?
<--- Score

289. What are the primary barriers to effective knowledge transfer in your organization?
<--- Score

290. How is agile project management applied in different domains outside of software industry?
<--- Score

291. Why should a formal modeling tool be used in project management?
<--- Score

292. How timely was the training you received in preparation for the use of the product/service?
<--- Score

293. What is different about ICT procurement?
<--- Score

294. What kind of project management support/ system are you using in your work today?
<--- Score

295. Who are the PMOs customers and stakeholders?
<--- Score

296. How is the performance of the procurement function assessed?
<--- Score

297. Where is the content?
<--- Score

298. How can you keep up the momentum?

<--- Score

299. Have all stakeholders been heard from?
<--- Score

300. What are the major economic factors influencing project management?
<--- Score

301. What are the objectives for project success?
<--- Score

302. How do you rate the efficiency of the software?
<--- Score

303. When do you stop?
<--- Score

304. Are there differences between the theoretical Critical Chain rules and principles and the application of CCPM at your organization?
<--- Score

305. When should design and construct procurement be used?
<--- Score

306. Does the use of agile project management require new contract models in order to be successful?
<--- Score

307. What are the requirements of a project management software?
<--- Score

308. Who is responsible to ensure that the knowledge, skills, and processes of project management are applied as needed by the project?
<--- Score

309. How could Gamification be applied to project management?
<--- Score

310. How simple is it for you to access to all the projects after logging in?
<--- Score

311. What opportunities and benefits will come from implementing Agile project management in the design phase of your projects?
<--- Score

312. How is it useful?
<--- Score

313. What kind of training/education is offered?
<--- Score

314. What longer-term strategy does your organization have to achieve procurement reform?
<--- Score

315. How would you describe your organization s project management culture?
<--- Score

316. What part of how legal projects are currently managed frustrates you the most?

<--- Score

317. How is project governance communicated and implemented in the projects you work on?
<--- Score

318. In this context of Project Management, what can you say about Scrum alignment with CMM?
<--- Score

319. What on the project worked well and was effective in the delivery of the product?
<--- Score

320. Which project management process simplifications are appropriate for your organization and which are not?
<--- Score

321. Certainty of time: is project completion of time important?
<--- Score

322. What might threaten the quality of the deliverables?
<--- Score

323. What are the metrics of success?
<--- Score

324. How do you get in/log in in the software?
<--- Score

325. What other activities (project planning, project management, customer status reviews, process improvement, etc.) will benefit from

measurement results?
<--- Score

326. Is this a new procurement or a repeat exercise?
<--- Score

327. Can you do the work better than the client?
<--- Score

328. What is the level of customer satisfaction?
<--- Score

329. How often do you patch production systems?
<--- Score

330. How do you help the constraint be more productive?
<--- Score

331. What do clients want?
<--- Score

332. Can traditional project management and agile development coexist?
<--- Score

333. Does your organization have a written pro bono policy?
<--- Score

334. What comes first: the project budget, or the project activities?
<--- Score

335. How have you communicated with team

members and stakeholders on other projects?
<--- Score

336. To whom is the information provided?
<--- Score

337. How long does each task take to complete?
<--- Score

338. How does a project manager manage the quality aspect of a project?
<--- Score

339. Are existing procedures adequate for monitoring the status of the project?
<--- Score

340. Who attends to change management and employee communications?
<--- Score

341. Think about the types of services you might be able to offer. What skills, experience, or other assets do you have that you can share?
<--- Score

342. How does your organization perceive CCPM ?
<--- Score

343. Are you providing value?
<--- Score

344. How is staffing for each project done?
<--- Score

345. With the emphasis placed on the importance

of self-managing teams, does IT Project Management have a role in Agile?

<--- Score

346. Do team members know roles and have they been trained to perform them?

<--- Score

347. Will the project fail if the change request is not executed?

<--- Score

348. What skills will you attain with this program?

<--- Score

349. Can agile project management be used in highly regulated industries (i.e., FAA, FDA, etc.)?

<--- Score

350. Are there other initiatives currently in place or anticipated that will affect this project?

<--- Score

351. What systems are/are not being replaced?

<--- Score

352. Does lean and agile project management help your organization in coping with project complexity?

<--- Score

353. When will there be further communications?

<--- Score

354. When Does Release Management Apply to Project Management?

<--- Score

355. Have any significant changes been made to the baseline during the past fiscal year?
<--- Score

356. How could you describe your dream project management software?
<--- Score

357. What are you trying to achieve with the project?
<--- Score

358. Who should be at the project team meetings?
<--- Score

359. How many hours of training (education) are necessary for occupants to retain emergency procedure information?
<--- Score

360. Does the software quality assurance (sqa) function have a management reporting channel separate from the software development project management?
<--- Score

361. Who has access to production systems?
<--- Score

362. How can social media be used to benefit project managers and teams?
<--- Score

363. What proportion of your project managers

are contract employees?

<--- Score

364. Consider the implications of NOT doing the project – what benefits would be missed?

<--- Score

365. Should you consider a new project management tool?

<--- Score

366. What is the role of Project Management Body of Knowledge?

<--- Score

367. What specific qualitative benefits will be realized?

<--- Score

368. Who is Project Champion?

<--- Score

369. What sort of measures are there for Project management?

<--- Score

370. What will replace project management?

<--- Score

371. If CCPM is better, why is not everyone doing it?

<--- Score

372. Do you have policies and procedures for responding to media inquires?

<--- Score

373. How little structure can you get away with?
<--- Score

374. Can your organization deliver?
<--- Score

375. How will the necessary core IT capabilities be integrated with business capabilities, such project management, and change management?
<--- Score

376. Do you have a team space for collocation?
<--- Score

377. What techniques and tools are used for project management?
<--- Score

378. What is the optimal team size to which Agile should be applied for the team to be effective?
<--- Score

379. What does the future hold?
<--- Score

380. Does this project support your organization vision?
<--- Score

Add up total points for this section:
_ _ _ _ _ = Total points for this section

Divided by: _ _ _ _ _ _ (number of statements answered) = _ _ _ _ _ _
Average score for this section

Transfer your score to the Project
Management Index at the beginning of
the Self-Assessment.

Project Management and Managing Projects, Criteria for Project Managers:

1.0 Initiating Process Group: Project Management

1. Will the Project Management project meet the client requirements, and will it achieve the business success criteria that justified doing the Project Management project in the first place?

2. During which stage of Risk planning are risks prioritized based on probability and impact?

3. Have you evaluated the teams performance and asked for feedback?

4. Are identified risks being monitored properly, are new risks arising during the Project Management project or are foreseen risks occurring?

5. When are the deliverables to be generated in each phase?

6. Have requirements been tested, approved, and fulfill the Project Management project scope?

7. Were escalated issues resolved promptly?

8. What were things that you need to improve?

9. Where must it be done?

10. Do you know all the stakeholders impacted by the Project Management project and what needs are?

11. Are the changes in your Project Management project being formally requested, analyzed, and

approved by the appropriate decision makers?

12. Did the Project Management project team have the right skills?

13. Do you understand the communication expectations for this Project Management project?

14. Are you properly tracking the progress of the Project Management project and communicating the status to stakeholders?

15. In which Project Management project management process group is the detailed Project Management project budget created?

16. What do you need to do?

17. Who is funding the Project Management project?

18. What will be the pressing issues of tomorrow?

19. Were resources available as planned?

20. When will the Project Management project be done?

1.1 Project Charter: Project Management

21. When?

22. Who manages integration?

23. Is time of the essence?

24. How much?

25. What is the business need?

26. Why do you manage integration?

27. What outcome, in measureable terms, are you hoping to accomplish?

28. How will you know a change is an improvement?

29. Who is the Project Management project Manager?

30. What are the assigned resources?

31. Why executive support?

32. Must Have?

33. Why have you chosen the aim you have set forth?

34. Why use a Project Management project charter?

35. What barriers do you predict to your success?

36. Success determination factors: how will the success of the Project Management project be determined from the customers perspective?

37. Major high-level milestone targets: what events measure progress?

38. What date will the task finish?

39. Why do you need to manage scope?

40. Where does all this information come from?

1.2 Stakeholder Register: Project Management

41. What is the power of the stakeholder?

42. How much influence do they have on the Project Management project?

43. What opportunities exist to provide communications?

44. How should employers make voices heard?

45. What are the major Project Management project milestones requiring communications or providing communications opportunities?

46. What & Why?

47. Who are the stakeholders?

48. Who wants to talk about Security?

49. How will reports be created?

50. How big is the gap?

51. Who is managing stakeholder engagement?

52. Is your organization ready for change?

1.3 Stakeholder Analysis Matrix: Project Management

53. Seasonality, weather effects?

54. What can the Project Management projects outcome be used for?

55. Could any of your organizations weaknesses seriously threaten development?

56. Why is it important to identify them?

57. What do people from other organizations see as your strengths?

58. Who determines value?

59. How does the Project Management project involve consultations or collaboration with other organizations?

60. Who will promote/support the Project Management project, provided that they are involved?

61. What is accountability in relation to the Project Management project?

62. Philosophy and values?

63. New technologies, services, ideas?

64. What are the mechanisms of public and social accountability, and how can they be made better?

65. Opponents; who are the opponents?

66. Which conditions out of the control of the management are crucial for the sustainability of its effects?

67. What are the opportunities for communication?

68. Cashflow, start-up cash-drain?

69. Effects on core activities, distraction?

70. Competitors vulnerabilities?

71. Insurmountable weaknesses?

72. Tactics: eg, surprise, major contracts?

2.0 Planning Process Group: Project Management

73. What will you do to minimize the impact should a risk event occur?

74. Are the follow-up indicators relevant and do they meet the quality needed to measure the outputs and outcomes of the Project Management project?

75. Why is it important to determine activity sequencing on Project Management projects?

76. To what extent has the intervention strategy been adapted to the areas of intervention in which it is being implemented?

77. Explanation: is what the Project Management project intents to solve a hard question?

78. Professionals want to know what is expected from them; what are the deliverables?

79. Does it make any difference if you are successful?

80. Are the necessary foundations in place to ensure the sustainability of the results of the Project Management project?

81. How will users learn how to use the deliverables?

82. What is the critical path for this Project Management project, and what is the duration of the

critical path?

83. Did the program design/ implementation strategy adequately address the planning stage necessary to set up structures, hire staff etc.?

84. What is involved in Project Management project scope management, and why is good Project Management project scope management so important on information technology Project Management projects?

85. What factors are contributing to progress or delay in the achievement of products and results?

86. To what extent are the participating departments coordinating with each other?

87. In which Project Management project management process group is the detailed Project Management project budget created?

88. Have operating capacities been created and/or reinforced in partners?

89. How should needs be met?

90. Just how important is your work to the overall success of the Project Management project?

91. Is the duration of the program sufficient to ensure a cycle that will Project Management project the sustainability of the interventions?

92. Is the Project Management project supported by national and/or local organizations?

2.1 Project Management Plan: Project Management

93. What would you do differently what did not work?

94. Are there any windfall benefits that would accrue to the Project Management project sponsor or other parties?

95. Has the selected plan been formulated using cost effectiveness and incremental analysis techniques?

96. Will you add a schedule and diagram?

97. What are the constraints?

98. Are there any client staffing expectations?

99. Is the engineering content at a feasibility level-of-detail, and is it sufficiently complete, to provide an adequate basis for the baseline cost estimate?

100. What are the training needs?

101. If the Project Management project management plan is a comprehensive document that guides you in Project Management project execution and control, then what should it NOT contain?

102. Are there non-structural buyout or relocation recommendations?

103. Are calculations and results of analyzes

essentially correct?

104. When is the Project Management project management plan created?

105. Are the proposed Project Management project purposes different than a previously authorized Project Management project?

106. What should you drop in order to add something new?

107. Are alternatives safe, functional, constructible, economical, reasonable and sustainable?

108. Why Change?

109. If the Project Management project is complex or scope is specialized, do you have appropriate and/or qualified staff available to perform the tasks?

2.2 Scope Management Plan: Project Management

110. Are you meeting with stake holders and team members?

111. What are the risks that could significantly affect the communication on the Project Management project?

112. Does the resource management plan include a personnel development plan?

113. Has a proper Project Management project work location been established that will allow the team to work together with user personnel?

114. Where do scope processes fit in?

115. Are tasks tracked by hours?

116. Has the scope management document been updated and distributed to help prevent scope creep?

117. Have the procedures for identifying budget variances been followed?

118. Have Project Management project success criteria been defined?

119. Does the Project Management project have a Statement of Work?

120. What happens to rejected deliverables?

121. For which criterion is it tolerable not to meet the original parameters?

122. Has a provision been made to reassess Project Management project risks at various Project Management project stages?

123. Do you have the reasons why the changes to your organizational systems and capabilities are required?

124. Are written status reports provided on a designated frequent basis?

125. Has the Project Management project approach and development strategy of the Project Management project been defined, documented and accepted by the appropriate stakeholders?

126. Given the scope of the Project Management project, which criterion should be optimized?

127. Alignment to strategic goals & objectives?

128. Are funding resource estimates sufficiently detailed and documented for use in planning and tracking the Project Management project?

2.3 Requirements Management Plan: Project Management

129. What are you counting on?

130. Who will do the reporting and to whom will reports be delivered?

131. Does the Project Management project have a Change Control process?

132. Do you understand the role that each stakeholder will play in the requirements process?

133. Will the product release be stable and mature enough to be deployed in the user community?

134. Is the system software (non-operating system) new to the IT Project Management project team?

135. What is the earliest finish date for this Project Management project if it is scheduled to start on ...?

136. What performance metrics will be used?

137. Is requirements work dependent on any other specific Project Management project or non-Project Management project activities (e.g. funding, approvals, procurement)?

138. What is a problem?

139. What information regarding the Project

Management project requirements will be reported?

140. Is there formal agreement on who has authority to approve a change in requirements?

141. Subject to change control?

142. What cost metrics will be used?

143. Has the requirements team been instructed in the Change Control process?

144. Are actual resource expenditures versus planned still acceptable?

145. How will you develop the schedule of requirements activities?

146. Which hardware or software, related to, or as outcome of the Project Management project is new to your organization?

147. How will unresolved questions be handled once approval has been obtained?

148. How knowledgeable is the team in the proposed application area?

2.4 Requirements Documentation: Project Management

149. What are current process problems?

150. Do technical resources exist?

151. Do your constraints stand?

152. How much does requirements engineering cost?

153. Are all functions required by the customer included?

154. How do you get the user to tell you what they want?

155. What marketing channels do you want to use: e-mail, letter or sms?

156. Does your organization restrict technical alternatives?

157. How will the proposed Project Management project help?

158. How linear / iterative is your Requirements Gathering process (or will it be)?

159. What will be the integration problems?

160. Can you check system requirements?

161. Who is interacting with the system?

162. How to document system requirements?

163. If applicable; are there issues linked with the fact that this is an offshore Project Management project?

164. Is the requirement properly understood?

165. What if the system wasn t implemented?

166. How does the proposed Project Management project contribute to the overall objectives of your organization?

167. What is effective documentation?

2.5 Requirements Traceability Matrix: Project Management

168. What percentage of Project Management projects are producing traceability matrices between requirements and other work products?

169. Why use a WBS?

170. How do you manage scope?

171. Do you have a clear understanding of all subcontracts in place?

172. Will you use a Requirements Traceability Matrix?

173. Is there a requirements traceability process in place?

174. What are the chronologies, contingencies, consequences, criteria?

175. Why do you manage scope?

176. What is the WBS?

177. Describe the process for approving requirements so they can be added to the traceability matrix and Project Management project work can be performed. Will the Project Management project requirements become approved in writing?

178. How small is small enough?

179. How will it affect the stakeholders personally in their career?

2.6 Project Scope Statement: Project Management

180. Will this process be communicated to the customer and Project Management project team?

181. Have the reports to be produced, distributed, and filed been defined?

182. Is the Project Management project sponsor function identified and defined?

183. Are there adequate Project Management project control systems?

184. How will you verify the accuracy of the work of the Project Management project, and what constitutes acceptance of the deliverables?

185. Have the configuration management functions been assigned?

186. What actions will be taken to mitigate the risk?

187. Has a method and process for requirement tracking been developed?

188. Is the plan for Project Management project resources adequate?

189. Is the Project Management project manager qualified and experienced in Project Management project management?

190. Is the change control process documented and on file?

191. Does the scope statement still need some clarity?

192. Project Management project lead, team lead, solution architect?

193. Are there specific processes you will use to evaluate and approve/reject changes?

194. Will the Project Management project risks be managed according to the Project Management projects risk management process?

195. Elements of scope management that deal with concept development ?

196. Risks?

197. Is this process communicated to the customer and team members?

198. Identify how your team and you will create the Project Management project scope statement and the work breakdown structure (WBS). Document how you will create the Project Management project scope statement and WBS, and make sure you answer the following questions: In defining Project Management project scope and the WBS, will you and your Project Management project team be using methods defined by your organization, methods defined by the Project Management project management office (PMO), or other methods?

2.7 Assumption and Constraint Log: Project Management

199. After observing execution of process, is it in compliance with the documented Plan?

200. Is the current scope of the Project Management project substantially different than that originally defined in the approved Project Management project plan?

201. Are you meeting your customers expectations consistently?

202. Are funding and staffing resource estimates sufficiently detailed and documented for use in planning and tracking the Project Management project?

203. What weaknesses do you have?

204. Diagrams and tables are included to account for complex concepts and increase overall readability?

205. Are there processes defining how software will be developed including development methods, overall timeline for development, software product standards, and traceability?

206. Contradictory information between different documents?

207. Do the requirements meet the standards of

correctness, completeness, consistency, accuracy, and readability?

208. Is the process working, and people are not executing in compliance of the process?

209. Contradictory information between document sections?

210. How do you design an auditing system?

211. Would known impacts serve as impediments?

212. Are best practices and metrics employed to identify issues, progress, performance, etc.?

213. How can you prevent/fix violations?

214. Should factors be unpredictable over time?

215. Was the document/deliverable developed per the appropriate or required standards (for example, Institute of Electrical and Electronics Engineers standards)?

216. Is the definition of the Project Management project scope clear; what needs to be accomplished?

217. Were the system requirements formally reviewed prior to initiating the design phase?

218. Are formal code reviews conducted?

2.8 Work Breakdown Structure: Project Management

219. How much detail?

220. When do you stop?

221. Who has to do it?

222. Is it a change in scope?

223. When would you develop a Work Breakdown Structure?

224. What is the probability that the Project Management project duration will exceed xx weeks?

225. Is the work breakdown structure (wbs) defined and is the scope of the Project Management project clear with assigned deliverable owners?

226. Is it still viable?

227. How big is a work-package?

228. Can you make it?

229. How many levels?

230. When does it have to be done?

231. Where does it take place?

232. How will you and your Project Management project team define the Project Management projects scope and work breakdown structure?

233. Do you need another level?

234. Why is it useful?

235. Why would you develop a Work Breakdown Structure?

236. How far down?

237. What has to be done?

238. What is the probability of completing the Project Management project in less that xx days?

2.9 WBS Dictionary: Project Management

239. Does the contractors system provide unit costs, equivalent unit or lot costs in terms of labor, material, other direct, and indirect costs?

240. Are indirect costs charged to the appropriate indirect pools and incurring organization?

241. Is budgeted cost for work performed calculated in a manner consistent with the way work is planned?

242. All cwbs elements specified for external reporting?

243. Does the contractor require sufficient detailed planning of control accounts to constrain the application of budget initially allocated for future effort to current effort?

244. Does the contractors system provide for the determination of cost variances attributable to the excess usage of material?

245. Are retroactive changes to direct costs and indirect costs prohibited except for the correction of errors and routine accounting adjustments?

246. Are overhead costs budgets established on a basis consistent with anticipated direct business base?

247. Where engineering standards or other internal work measurement systems are used, is there a formal relationship between corresponding values and work package budgets?

248. The total budget for the contract (including estimates for authorized and unpriced work)?

249. Appropriate work authorization documents which subdivide the contractual effort and responsibilities, within functional organizations?

250. Changes in the overhead pool and/or organization structures?

251. Are data being used by managers in an effective manner to ascertain Project Management project or functional status, to identify reasons or significant variance, and to initiate appropriate corrective action?

252. Are the wbs and organizational levels for application of the Project Management projected overhead costs identified?

253. Are significant decision points, constraints, and interfaces identified as key milestones?

254. What is the end result of a work package?

255. Are estimates of costs at completion utilized in determining contract funding requirements and reporting them?

256. Are authorized changes being incorporated in a timely manner?

257. Are the responsibilities and authorities of each of the above organizational elements or managers clearly defined?

258. Are work packages reasonably short in time duration or do they have adequate objective indicators/milestones to minimize subjectivity of the in process work evaluation?

2.10 Schedule Management Plan: Project Management

259. Are cause and effect determined for risks when they occur?

260. Are any non-compliance issues that exist due to your organizations practices communicated to your organization?

261. Is quality monitored from the perspective of the customers needs and expectations?

262. Has a structured approach been used to break work effort into manageable components (WBS)?

263. Is pert / critical path or equivalent methodology being used?

264. What threats might prevent you from getting there?

265. Have activity relationships and interdependencies within tasks been adequately identified?

266. Have adequate resources been provided by management to ensure Project Management project success?

267. Is your organization certified as a broker of the products/supplies?

268. Is a process for scheduling and reporting defined, including forms and formats?

269. Have stakeholder accountabilities & responsibilities been clearly defined?

270. Does the ims reflect accurate current status and credible start/finish forecasts for all to-go tasks and milestones?

271. Identify the amount of schedule variation that triggers a warning. What happens if a warning is triggered?

272. Are the constraints or deadlines associated with the task accurate?

273. Are post milestone Project Management project reviews (PMPR) conducted with your organization at least once a year?

274. Pareto diagrams, statistical sampling, flow charting or trend analysis used quality monitoring?

275. Will rolling way planning be used?

276. Why time management?

2.11 Activity List: Project Management

277. How can the Project Management project be displayed graphically to better visualize the activities?

278. How will it be performed?

279. What is the probability the Project Management project can be completed in xx weeks?

280. What is your organizations history in doing similar activities?

281. Should you include sub-activities?

282. What is the LF and LS for each activity?

283. Are the required resources available or need to be acquired?

284. How much slack is available in the Project Management project?

285. What will be performed?

286. Where will it be performed?

287. When will the work be performed?

288. For other activities, how much delay can be tolerated?

289. How should ongoing costs be monitored to try to keep the Project Management project within budget?

290. The wbs is developed as part of a joint planning session. and how do you know that youhave done this right?

291. How difficult will it be to do specific activities on this Project Management project?

292. Is infrastructure setup part of your Project Management project?

293. What went right?

294. What are the critical bottleneck activities?

295. How detailed should a Project Management project get?

2.12 Activity Attributes: Project Management

296. Can you re-assign any activities to another resource to resolve an over-allocation?

297. Resources to accomplish the work?

298. Can more resources be added?

299. Time for overtime?

300. Where else does it apply?

301. What went wrong?

302. What activity do you think you should spend the most time on?

303. How difficult will it be to do specific activities on this Project Management project?

304. Have you identified the Activity Leveling Priority code value on each activity?

305. How else could the items be grouped?

306. Would you consider either of corresponding activities an outlier?

307. Is there anything planned that does not need to be here?

308. How many days do you need to complete the work scope with a limit of X number of resources?

309. Does your organization of the data change its meaning?

310. Resource is assigned to?

311. How do you manage time?

312. Are the required resources available?

313. Were there other ways you could have organized the data to achieve similar results?

2.13 Milestone List: Project Management

314. Describe the concept of the technology, product or service that will be or has been developed. How will it be used?

315. Identify critical paths (one or more) and which activities are on the critical path?

316. Obstacles faced?

317. Timescales, deadlines and pressures?

318. How late can the activity finish?

319. Loss of key staff?

320. Vital contracts and partners?

321. Gaps in capabilities?

322. New USPs?

323. It is to be a narrative text providing the crucial aspects of your Project Management project proposal answering what, who, how, when and where?

324. Environmental effects?

325. How will the milestone be verified?

326. Usps (unique selling points)?

327. How difficult will it be to do specific activities on this Project Management project?

328. Own known vulnerabilities?

329. Describe the industry you are in and the market growth opportunities. What is the market for your technology, product or service?

2.14 Network Diagram: Project Management

330. What to do and When?

331. Planning: who, how long, what to do?

332. What activities must occur simultaneously with this activity?

333. What are the Key Success Factors?

334. What is the probability of completing the Project Management project in less that xx days?

335. Are the gantt chart and/or network diagram updated periodically and used to assess the overall Project Management project timetable?

336. What job or jobs follow it?

337. Why must you schedule milestones, such as reviews, throughout the Project Management project?

338. What are the tools?

339. What activity must be completed immediately before this activity can start?

340. Can you calculate the confidence level?

341. Review the logical flow of the network diagram.

Take a look at which activities you have first and then sequence the activities. Do they make sense?

342. Are you on time?

343. Will crashing x weeks return more in benefits than it costs?

344. If the Project Management project network diagram cannot change and you have extra personnel resources, what is the BEST thing to do?

345. What is the lowest cost to complete this Project Management project in xx weeks?

346. Which type of network diagram allows you to depict four types of dependencies?

347. What are the Major Administrative Issues?

2.15 Activity Resource Requirements: Project Management

348. What is the Work Plan Standard?

349. Which logical relationship does the PDM use most often?

350. When does monitoring begin?

351. How do you handle petty cash?

352. What are constraints that you might find during the Human Resource Planning process?

353. Do you use tools like decomposition and rolling-wave planning to produce the activity list and other outputs?

354. How many signatures do you require on a check and does this match what is in your policy and procedures?

355. Are there unresolved issues that need to be addressed?

356. Why do you do that?

357. Other support in specific areas?

358. Organizational Applicability?

359. Anything else?

2.16 Resource Breakdown Structure: Project Management

360. Who delivers the information?

361. How should the information be delivered?

362. Which resource planning tool provides information on resource responsibility and accountability?

363. When do they need the information?

364. How can this help you with team building?

365. What can you do to improve productivity?

366. Who needs what information?

367. Is predictive resource analysis being done?

368. Who will use the system?

369. The list could probably go on, but, the thing that you would most like to know is, How long & How much?

370. Goals for the Project Management project. What is each stakeholders desired outcome for the Project Management project?

371. Why do you do it?

372. What is the difference between % Complete and % work?

373. Who will be used as a Project Management project team member?

374. What are the requirements for resource data?

2.17 Activity Duration Estimates: Project Management

375. Are steps identified by which Project Management project documents may be changed?

376. If the optimiztic estimate for an activity is 12days, and the pessimistic estimate is 18days, what is the standard deviation of this activity?

377. Why do you need a good WBS to use Project Management project management software?

378. What are the main types of contracts if you do decide to outsource?

379. Does a process exist to identify Project Management project roles, responsibilities and reporting relationships?

380. Do checklists exist that list frequently performed activities?

381. Will new hardware or software be required for servers or client machines?

382. Based on , if you need to shorten the duration of the Project Management project, what activity would you try to shorten?

383. Which tips for taking the PMP exam do you think would be most helpful for you?

384. If you plan to take the PMP exam soon, what should you do to prepare?

385. Which would be the NEXT thing for the Project Management project manager to do?

386. Does a process exist to determine the probability of risk events?

387. Will the new application negatively affect the current IT infrastructure?

388. What is the difference between using brainstorming and the Delphi technique for risk identification?

389. Research risk management software. Are many products available?

390. What steps did your organization take to earn this prestigious quality award?

391. Consider the history of modern quality management. How have experts such as Deming, Juran, Crosby, and Taguchi affected the quality movement and todays use of Six Sigma?

392. Calculate the expected duration for an activity that has a most likely time of 5, a pessimistic time of 13, and a optimiztic time of 3?

393. Is risk identification completed regularly throughout the Project Management project?

2.18 Duration Estimating Worksheet: Project Management

394. What work will be included in the Project Management project?

395. Do any colleagues have experience with your organization and/or RFPs?

396. When do the individual activities need to start and finish?

397. When does your organization expect to be able to complete it?

398. Is a construction detail attached (to aid in explanation)?

399. Done before proceeding with this activity or what can be done concurrently?

400. When, then?

401. What questions do you have?

402. What is an Average Project Management project?

403. Will the Project Management project collaborate with the local community and leverage resources?

404. Science = process: remember the scientific method?

405. How can the Project Management project be displayed graphically to better visualize the activities?

406. How should ongoing costs be monitored to try to keep the Project Management project within budget?

407. Is this operation cost effective?

408. What utility impacts are there?

409. Why estimate costs?

410. Why estimate time and cost?

2.19 Project Schedule: Project Management

411. If there are any qualifying green components to this Project Management project, what portion of the total Project Management project cost is green?

412. Are procedures defined by which the Project Management project schedule may be changed?

413. Meet requirements?

414. Are quality inspections and review activities listed in the Project Management project schedule(s)?

415. Is the structure for tracking the Project Management project schedule well defined and assigned to a specific individual?

416. What is the purpose of a Project Management project schedule?

417. How can slack be negative?

418. Did the Project Management project come in on schedule?

419. What documents, if any, will the subcontractor provide (eg Project Management project schedule, quality plan etc)?

420. Why or why not?

421. How can you address that situation?

422. How detailed should a Project Management project get?

423. How do you know that youhave done this right?

424. How effectively were issues able to be resolved without impacting the Project Management project Schedule or Budget?

425. Master Project Management project schedule?

426. Activity charts and bar charts are graphical representations of a Project Management project schedule ...how do they differ?

2.20 Cost Management Plan: Project Management

427. Cost / benefit analysis?

428. Have Project Management project team accountabilities & responsibilities been clearly defined?

429. Does a documented Project Management project organizational policy & plan (i.e. governance model) exist?

430. Are the payment terms being followed?

431. Sensitivity analysis?

432. Is Project Management project work proceeding in accordance with the original Project Management project schedule?

433. Has the Project Management project manager been identified?

434. Does the schedule include Project Management project management time and change request analysis time?

435. Mitigation – based on the action, cost and probability of success, will the mitigation be made?

436. Is documentation created for communication with the suppliers and Vendors?

437. For cost control purposes?

438. Eac -estimate at completion, what is the total job expected to cost?

439. Does the detailed work plan match the complexity of tasks with the capabilities of personnel?

440. Are the people assigned to the Project Management project sufficiently qualified?

441. Weve met your goals?

442. What does this mean to a cost or scheduler manager?

2.21 Activity Cost Estimates: Project Management

443. How do you fund change orders?

444. What is the Project Management projects sustainability strategy that will ensure Project Management project results will endure or be sustained?

445. Certification of actual expenditures?

446. Performance bond should always provide what part of the contract value?

447. The impact and what actions were taken?

448. How and when do you enter into Project Management project Procurement Management?

449. What happens if you cannot produce the documentation for the single audit?

450. Did the Project Management project team have the right skills?

451. Are data needed on characteristics of care?

452. Are cost subtotals needed?

453. What makes a good expected result statement?

454. What is a Project Management project

Management Plan?

455. How do you allocate indirect costs to activities?

456. What are you looking for?

457. How do you do activity recasts?

458. Can you delete activities or make them inactive?

459. Padding is bad and contingencies are good. what is the difference?

460. What were things that you did well, and could improve, and how?

461. Review – what are some common errors in activities to avoid?

2.22 Cost Estimating Worksheet: Project Management

462. Does the Project Management project provide innovative ways for stakeholders to overcome obstacles or deliver better outcomes?

463. Will the Project Management project collaborate with the local community and leverage resources?

464. What additional Project Management project(s) could be initiated as a result of this Project Management project?

465. Can a trend be established from historical performance data on the selected measure and are the criteria for using trend analysis or forecasting methods met?

466. Value pocket identification & quantification what are value pockets?

467. Who is best positioned to know and assist in identifying corresponding factors?

468. What will others want?

469. What is the purpose of estimating?

470. What happens to any remaining funds not used?

471. Is it feasible to establish a control group arrangement?

472. Identify the timeframe necessary to monitor progress and collect data to determine how the selected measure has changed?

473. Is the Project Management project responsive to community need?

474. How will the results be shared and to whom?

475. What info is needed?

476. What is the estimated labor cost today based upon this information?

477. What costs are to be estimated?

478. What can be included?

479. Ask: are others positioned to know, are others credible, and will others cooperate?

2.23 Cost Baseline: Project Management

480. Why do you manage cost?

481. Impact to environment?

482. Have you identified skills that are missing from your team?

483. On budget?

484. How do you manage cost?

485. Has the Project Management projected annual cost to operate and maintain the product(s) or service(s) been approved and funded?

486. What is it ?

487. What deliverables come first?

488. Pcs for your new business. what would the life cycle costs be?

489. Have all approved changes to the schedule baseline been identified and impact on the Project Management project documented?

490. Has the documentation relating to operation and maintenance of the product(s) or service(s) been delivered to, and accepted by, operations management?

491. Has operations management formally accepted responsibility for operating and maintaining the product(s) or service(s) delivered by the Project Management project?

492. Has the Project Management project documentation been archived or otherwise disposed as described in the Project Management project communication plan?

493. Is there anything unique in this Project Management projects scope statement that will affect resources?

494. Who will use corresponding metrics ?

495. What does a good WBS NOT look like?

496. Have all approved changes to the cost baseline been identified and impact on the Project Management project documented?

497. Have the actual milestone completion dates been compared to the approved schedule?

498. If you sold 10x widgets on a day, what would the affect on profits be?

2.24 Quality Management Plan: Project Management

499. How does your organization design processes to ensure others meet customer and others requirements?

500. Are there processes in place to ensure internal consistency between the source code components?

501. What are you trying to accomplish?

502. Does the program use other agents to collect samples?

503. Have all necessary approvals been obtained?

504. Were the right locations/samples tested for the right parameters?

505. Are there unnecessary steps that are creating bottlenecks and/or causing people to wait?

506. How will you know that a change is actually an improvement?

507. Methodology followed?

508. How effectively was the Quality Management Plan applied during Project Management project Execution?

509. How long do you retain data?

510. Are you following the quality standards?

511. How many Project Management project staff does this specific process affect?

512. How do your action plans support the strategic objectives?

513. How is staff trained?

514. Do you periodically review your data quality system to see that it is up to date and appropriate?

515. List your organizations customer contact standards that employees are expected to maintain. How are corresponding standards measured?

516. With the five whys method, the team considers why the issue being explored occurred. do others then take that initial answer and ask why?

2.25 Quality Metrics: Project Management

517. What about still open problems?

518. Were quality attributes reported?

519. Which report did you use to create the data you are submitting?

520. Was review conducted per standard protocols?

521. What if the biggest risk to your business were the already stated people who do not complain?

522. Are quality metrics defined?

523. What approved evidence based screening tools can be used?

524. Has risk analysis been adequately reviewed?

525. How are requirements conflicts resolved?

526. Did evaluation start on time?

527. Has it met internal or external standards?

528. The metrics–what is being considered?

529. How exactly do you define when differences exist?

530. What can manufacturing professionals do to ensure quality is seen as an integral part of the entire product lifecycle?

531. Were number of defects identified?

532. Is material complete (and does it meet the standards)?

533. What level of statistical confidence do you use?

534. Can visual measures help you to filter visualizations of interest?

535. Which data do others need in one place to target areas of improvement?

2.26 Process Improvement Plan: Project Management

536. Purpose of goal: the motive is determined by asking, why do you want to achieve this goal?

537. Why do you want to achieve the goal?

538. Where do you focus?

539. Have storage and access mechanisms and procedures been determined?

540. Modeling current processes is great, and will you ever see a return on that investment?

541. What is the test-cycle concept?

542. How do you measure?

543. Management commitment at all levels?

544. Are you making progress on the goals?

545. What actions are needed to address the problems and achieve the goals?

546. Does explicit definition of the measures exist?

547. How do you manage quality?

548. Has the time line required to move measurement results from the points of collection to databases or

users been established?

549. Are you meeting the quality standards?

550. Where are you now?

551. What personnel are the change agents for your initiative?

552. Does your process ensure quality?

553. What personnel are the sponsors for that initiative?

554. What personnel are the champions for the initiative?

555. What is quality and how will you ensure it?

2.27 Responsibility Assignment Matrix: Project Management

556. Performance to date and material commitment?

557. What are the deliverables?

558. What expertise is not available in your department?

559. Time-phased control account budgets?

560. Are all authorized tasks assigned to identified organizational elements?

561. Can the contractor substantiate work package and planning package budgets?

562. Evaluate the performance of operating organizations?

563. What is the number one predictor of a groups productivity?

564. Are people afraid to let you know when others are under allocated?

565. What is the justification?

566. Is every signing-off responsibility and every communicating responsibility critically necessary?

567. Undistributed budgets, if any?

568. Is work progressively subdivided into detailed work packages as requirements are defined?

569. What do people write/say on status/Project Management project reports?

570. Are there any drawbacks to using a responsibility assignment matrix?

571. The staff interests – is the group or the person interested in working for this Project Management project?

572. Evaluate the impact of schedule changes, work around, etc?

573. What are the known stakeholder requirements?

2.28 Roles and Responsibilities: Project Management

574. Does the team have access to and ability to use data analysis tools?

575. What should you do now to prepare yourself for a promotion, increased responsibilities or a different job?

576. What areas would you highlight for changes or improvements?

577. To decide whether to use a quality measurement, ask how will you know when it is achieved?

578. What areas of supervision are challenging for you?

579. How is your work-life balance?

580. Was the expectation clearly communicated?

581. Who is involved?

582. What are your major roles and responsibilities in the area of performance measurement and assessment?

583. Attainable / achievable: the goal is attainable; can you actually accomplish the goal?

584. Be specific; avoid generalities. Thank you and

great work alone are insufficient. What exactly do you appreciate and why?

585. What should you do now to prepare for your career 5+ years from now?

586. Implementation of actions: Who are the responsible units?

587. What expectations were NOT met?

588. How well did the Project Management project Team understand the expectations of specific roles and responsibilities?

589. What should you do now to ensure that you are exceeding expectations and excelling in your current position?

590. What is working well?

591. Are governance roles and responsibilities documented?

592. Does your vision/mission support a culture of quality data?

593. What is working well within your organizations performance management system?

2.29 Human Resource Management Plan: Project Management

594. Does the business case include how the Project Management project aligns with your organizations strategic goals & objectives?

595. Are the Project Management project plans updated on a frequent basis?

596. How can below standard performers be guided/developed to upgrade performance?

597. Do Project Management project teams & team members report on status / activities / progress?

598. Are the right people being attracted and retained to meet the future challenges?

599. Project Management project Objectives?

600. Are mitigation strategies identified?

601. Are parking lot items captured?

602. Is your organization primarily focused on a specific industry?

603. Are changes in deliverable commitments agreed to by all affected groups & individuals?

604. Are the schedule estimates reasonable given the Project Management project?

605. Are people being developed to meet the challenges of the future?

606. Has the schedule been baselined?

607. Are cause and effect determined for risks when others occur?

608. Who will be impacted (both positively and negatively) as a result of or during the execution of this Project Management project?

609. Are target dates established for each milestone deliverable?

610. Is current scope of the Project Management project substantially different than that originally defined?

2.30 Communications Management Plan: Project Management

611. Which team member will work with each stakeholder?

612. What steps can you take for a positive relationship?

613. What to know?

614. Why do you manage communications?

615. Who will use or be affected by the result of a Project Management project?

616. Where do team members get information?

617. Are you constantly rushing from meeting to meeting?

618. Do you feel a register helps?

619. How did the term stakeholder originate?

620. In your work, how much time is spent on stakeholder identification?

621. What communications method?

622. Timing: when do the effects of the communication take place?

623. Are stakeholders internal or external?

624. Why manage stakeholders?

625. How do you manage communications?

626. How often do you engage with stakeholders?

627. How will the person responsible for executing the communication item be notified?

628. Do you have members of your team responsible for certain stakeholders?

629. What to learn?

630. Which stakeholders can influence others?

2.31 Risk Management Plan: Project Management

631. Are there alternative opinions/solutions/ processes you should explore?

632. Monitoring -what factors can you track that will enable you to determine if the risk is becoming more or less likely?

633. Litigation – what is the probability that lawsuits will cause problems or delays in the Project Management project?

634. Are the best people available?

635. People risk -are people with appropriate skills available to help complete the Project Management project?

636. Can it be changed quickly?

637. Are the participants able to keep up with the workload?

638. Is Project Management project scope stable?

639. Is there additional information that would make you more confident about your analysis?

640. What is the impact to the Project Management project if the item is not resolved in a timely fashion?

641. How can the process be made more effective or less cumbersome (process improvements)?

642. Financial risk -can your organization afford to undertake the Project Management project?

643. Do requirements put excessive performance constraints on the product?

644. Is a software Project Management project management tool available?

645. How much risk can you tolerate?

646. Are flexibility and reuse paramount?

647. What should be done with non-critical risks?

648. Are formal technical reviews part of this process?

649. Is the customer willing to establish rapid communication links with the developer?

650. Have staff received necessary training?

2.32 Risk Register: Project Management

651. What could prevent you delivering on the strategic program objectives and what is being done to mitigate corresponding issues?

652. Risk probability and impact: how will the probabilities and impacts of risk items be assessed?

653. Having taken action, how did the responses effect change, and where is the Project Management project now?

654. What is your current and future risk profile?

655. Assume the event happens, what is the Most Likely impact?

656. What are you going to do to limit the Project Management projects risk exposure due to the identified risks?

657. Preventative actions - planned actions to reduce the likelihood a risk will occur and/or reduce the seriousness should it occur. What should you do now?

658. How well are risks controlled?

659. Recovery actions - planned actions taken once a risk has occurred to allow you to move on. What should you do after?

660. Who is accountable?

661. What may happen or not go according to plan?

662. Which key risks have ineffective responses or outstanding improvement actions?

663. What are the main aims, objectives of the policy, strategy, or service and the intended outcomes?

664. Are your objectives at risk?

665. How are risks graded?

666. Are there any gaps in the evidence?

667. What should you do when?

668. When would you develop a risk register?

669. User involvement: do you have the right users?

2.33 Probability and Impact Assessment: Project Management

670. Does the customer have a solid idea of what is required?

671. How would you assess the risk management process in the Project Management project?

672. What kind of preparation would be required to do this?

673. What will be the likely political situation during the life of the Project Management project?

674. What is the risk appetite?

675. Do you have a consistent repeatable process that is actually used?

676. Do you use any methods to analyze risks?

677. Is the process supported by tools?

678. Are requirements fully understood by the software engineering team and customers?

679. How are the local factors going to affect the absorption?

680. What new technologies are being explored in the same area?

681. Are testing tools available and suitable?

682. Are tool mentors available?

683. Are tools for analysis and design available?

684. Do the people have the right combinations of skills?

685. Are there new risks that mitigation strategies might introduce?

686. When and how will the recent breakthroughs in basic research lead to commercial products?

687. What significant shift will occur in governmental policies, laws, and regulations pertaining to specific industries?

688. Is the Project Management project cutting across the entire organization?

689. How much risk do others need to take?

2.34 Probability and Impact Matrix: Project Management

690. Amount of reused software?

691. Who should be notified of the occurrence of each of the risk indicators?

692. How solid is the Project Management projection of competitive reaction?

693. What has the Project Management project manager forgotten to do?

694. What risks are necessary to achieve success?

695. Risk categorization -which of your categories has more risk than others?

696. What are the risks involved in appointing external agencies to manage the Project Management project?

697. How well were you able to manage your risk?

698. How can you understand and diagnose risks and identify sources?

699. Do you manage the process through use of metrics?

700. Have top software and customer managers formally committed to support the Project Management project?

701. Which phase of the Project Management project do you take part in?

702. What are the probable external agencies to act as Project Management project manager?

703. Why do you need to manage Project Management project Risk?

704. What will be cost of redeployment of the personnel?

705. What will be the likely incidence of conflict with neighboring Project Management projects?

706. How are you working with risks?

2.35 Risk Data Sheet: Project Management

707. Whom do you serve (customers)?

708. What can you do?

709. Potential for recurrence?

710. If it happens, what are the consequences?

711. Are new hazards created?

712. What was measured?

713. What can happen?

714. How reliable is the data source?

715. What if client refuses?

716. Has a sensitivity analysis been carried out?

717. What is the environment within which you operate (social trends, economic, community values, broad based participation, national directions etc.)?

718. What are you trying to achieve (Objectives)?

719. Who has a vested interest in how you perform as your organization (our stakeholders)?

720. Type of risk identified?

721. What are the main threats to your existence?

722. What is the chance that it will happen?

723. Risk of what?

724. Is the data sufficiently specified in terms of the type of failure being analyzed, and its frequency or probability?

725. What is the duration of infection (the length of time the host is infected with the organizm) in a normal healthy human host?

726. What are you weak at and therefore need to do better?

2.36 Procurement Management Plan: Project Management

727. Is stakeholder involvement adequate?

728. Is a payment system in place with proper reviews and approvals?

729. Have the key elements of a coherent Project Management project management strategy been established?

730. Has a quality assurance plan been developed for the Project Management project?

731. Is there a procurement management plan in place?

732. Were sponsors and decision makers available when needed outside regularly scheduled meetings?

733. Are all payments made according to the contract(s)?

734. Is there a formal set of procedures supporting Issues Management?

735. Are key risk mitigation strategies added to the Project Management project schedule?

736. Are the results of quality assurance reviews provided to affected groups & individuals?

737. What areas are overlooked on this Project Management project?

738. Are quality inspections and review activities listed in the Project Management project schedule(s)?

739. Is there a formal process for updating the Project Management project baseline?

740. Are the Project Management project plans updated on a frequent basis?

741. Does the Project Management project team have the right skills?

742. What types of contracts will be used?

2.37 Source Selection Criteria: Project Management

743. How do you facilitate evaluation against published criteria?

744. What information is to be provided and when should it be provided?

745. What can not be disclosed?

746. Who is entitled to a debriefing?

747. In order of importance, which evaluation criteria are the most critical to the determination of your overall rating?

748. Who should attend debriefings?

749. Are there any specific considerations that precludes offers from being selected as the awardee?

750. How are oral presentations documented?

751. How do you consolidate reviews and analysis of evaluators?

752. What risks were identified in the proposals?

753. How should the oral presentations be handled?

754. Can you reasonably estimate total organization requirements for the coming year?

755. How should oral presentations be prepared for?

756. How long will it take for the purchase cost to be the same as the lease cost?

757. Why promote competition?

758. What should preproposal conferences accomplish?

759. Has all proposal data been loaded?

760. Team leads: what is your process for assigning ratings?

761. Do you consider all weaknesses, significant weaknesses, and deficiencies?

762. How are clarifications and communications appropriately used?

2.38 Stakeholder Management Plan: Project Management

763. Does a documented Project Management project organizational policy & plan (i.e. governance model) exist?

764. Were Project Management project team members involved in the development of activity & task decomposition?

765. Have all involved stakeholders and work groups committed to the Project Management project?

766. Are corrective actions and variances reported?

767. Is the Project Management project sponsor clearly communicating the business case or rationale for why this Project Management project is needed?

768. Are schedule deliverables actually delivered?

769. Are there cosmetic errors that hinder readability and comprehension?

770. Which of the records created within the Project Management project, if any, does the Business Owner require access to?

771. Does the role of the Project Management project Team cease upon the delivery of the Project Management projects outputs?

772. Are there checklists created to demine if all quality processes are followed?

773. Has a quality assurance plan been developed for the Project Management project?

774. Have the key functions and capabilities been defined and assigned to each release or iteration?

775. Is the quality assurance team identified?

776. Has a Project Management project Communications Plan been developed?

777. What records are required (eg purchase orders, agreements)?

778. Are metrics used to evaluate and manage Vendors?

779. Are trade-offs between accepting the risk and mitigating the risk identified?

780. Are issues raised, assessed, actioned, and resolved in a timely and efficient manner?

2.39 Change Management Plan: Project Management

781. Who will do the training?

782. How much Project Management project management is needed?

783. Has the priority for this Project Management project been set by the Business Unit Management Team?

784. Is there support for this application(s) and are the details available for distribution?

785. Have the approved procedures and policies been published?

786. Would you need to tailor a special message for each segment of the audience?

787. How much change management is needed?

788. How frequently should you repeat the message?

789. What is the reason for the communication?

790. Do there need to be new channels developed?

791. What will be the preferred method of delivery?

792. How do you gain sponsors buy-in to the communication plan?

793. What are the responsibilities assigned to each role?

794. Has the training co-ordinator been provided with the training details and put in place the necessary arrangements?

795. When should a given message be communicated?

796. Will all field readiness criteria have been practically met prior to training roll-out?

797. Who in the business it includes?

798. What is the most cynical response it can receive?

799. What would be an estimate of the total cost for the activities required to carry out the change initiative?

800. Why is it important?

3.0 Executing Process Group: Project Management

801. Contingency planning. if a risk event occurs, what will you do?

802. How can software assist in procuring goods and services?

803. What are the key components of the Project Management project communications plan?

804. In what way has the program come up with innovative measures for problem-solving?

805. After how many days will the lease cost be the same as the purchase cost for the equipment?

806. Who will be the main sponsor?

807. Measurable - are the targets measurable?

808. How does a Project Management project life cycle differ from a product life cycle?

809. Just how important is your work to the overall success of the Project Management project?

810. What areas were overlooked on this Project Management project?

811. How can you use Microsoft Project Management project and Excel to assist in Project Management

project risk management?

812. What are the typical Project Management project management skills?

813. On which process should team members spend the most time?

814. What type of people would you want on your team?

815. What are the main processes included in Project Management project quality management?

816. Specific - is the objective clear in terms of what, how, when, and where the situation will be changed?

817. How do you prevent staff are just doing busywork to pass the time?

818. How well did the chosen processes fit the needs of the Project Management project?

3.1 Team Member Status Report: Project Management

819. What specific interest groups do you have in place?

820. How can you make it practical?

821. Are your organizations Project Management projects more successful over time?

822. Does every department have to have a Project Management project Manager on staff?

823. Are the products of your organizations Project Management projects meeting customers objectives?

824. Do you have an Enterprise Project Management project Management Office (EPMO)?

825. Are the attitudes of staff regarding Project Management project work improving?

826. Why is it to be done?

827. How much risk is involved?

828. What is to be done?

829. The problem with Reward & Recognition Programs is that the truly deserving people all too often get left out. How can you make it practical?

830. Does the product, good, or service already exist within your organization?

831. When a teams productivity and success depend on collaboration and the efficient flow of information, what generally fails them?

832. How will resource planning be done?

833. Is there evidence that staff is taking a more professional approach toward management of your organizations Project Management projects?

834. How does this product, good, or service meet the needs of the Project Management project and your organization as a whole?

835. How it is to be done?

836. Will the staff do training or is that done by a third party?

837. Does your organization have the means (staff, money, contract, etc.) to produce or to acquire the product, good, or service?

3.2 Change Request: Project Management

838. Why do you want to have a change control system?

839. What type of changes does change control take into account?

840. What is a Change Request Form?

841. What should be regulated in a change control operating instruction?

842. How shall the implementation of changes be recorded?

843. Has a formal technical review been conducted to assess technical correctness?

844. Since there are no change requests in your Project Management project at this point, what must you have before you begin?

845. How do team members communicate with each other?

846. What is the function of the change control committee?

847. Which requirements attributes affect the risk to reliability the most?

848. Will there be a change request form in use?

849. Have scm procedures for noting the change, recording it, and reporting it been followed?

850. Why control change across the life cycle?

851. How are changes requested (forms, method of communication)?

852. What kind of information about the change request needs to be captured?

853. What must be taken into consideration when introducing change control programs?

854. Change request coordination ?

855. How fast will change requests be approved?

856. Who is included in the change control team?

857. Screen shots or attachments included in a Change Request?

3.3 Change Log: Project Management

858. Is the change backward compatible without limitations?

859. Is this a mandatory replacement?

860. Is the change request open, closed or pending?

861. Will the Project Management project fail if the change request is not executed?

862. Who initiated the change request?

863. When was the request approved?

864. Does the suggested change request represent a desired enhancement to the products functionality?

865. Is the change request within Project Management project scope?

866. Where do changes come from?

867. Is the requested change request a result of changes in other Project Management project(s)?

868. Should a more thorough impact analysis be conducted?

869. Do the described changes impact on the integrity or security of the system?

870. How does this change affect scope?

871. Is the submitted change a new change or a modification of a previously approved change?

872. When was the request submitted?

873. How does this relate to the standards developed for specific business processes?

874. How does this change affect the timeline of the schedule?

875. Does the suggested change request seem to represent a necessary enhancement to the product?

3.4 Decision Log: Project Management

876. Is your opponent open to a non-traditional workflow, or will it likely challenge anything you do?

877. How does provision of information, both in terms of content and presentation, influence acceptance of alternative strategies?

878. How does the use a Decision Support System influence the strategies/tactics or costs?

879. What was the rationale for the decision?

880. What is your overall strategy for quality control / quality assurance procedures?

881. Which variables make a critical difference?

882. Does anything need to be adjusted?

883. What is the line where eDiscovery ends and document review begins?

884. With whom was the decision shared or considered?

885. How does an increasing emphasis on cost containment influence the strategies and tactics used?

886. What alternatives/risks were considered?

887. It becomes critical to track and periodically revisit both operational effectiveness; Are you noticing all that you need to, and are you interpreting what you see effectively?

888. What eDiscovery problem or issue did your organization set out to fix or make better?

889. What makes you different or better than others companies selling the same thing?

890. Who is the decisionmaker?

891. How consolidated and comprehensive a story can you tell by capturing currently available incident data in a central location and through a log of key decisions during an incident?

892. How do you know when you are achieving it?

893. Decision-making process; how will the team make decisions?

894. Who will be given a copy of this document and where will it be kept?

895. Adversarial environment. is your opponent open to a non-traditional workflow, or will it likely challenge anything you do?

3.5 Quality Audit: Project Management

896. How does your organization know that its system for inducting new staff to maximize workplace contributions are appropriately effective and constructive?

897. Are there sufficient personnel having the necessary education, background, training, and experience to assure that all operations are correctly performed?

898. How does your organization know that its staff entrance standards are appropriately effective and constructive and being implemented consistently?

899. Do prior clients have a positive opinion of your organization?

900. How do staff know if they are doing a good job?

901. How does your organization know that its staff support services planning and management systems are appropriately effective and constructive?

902. How does your organization know that its security arrangements are appropriately effective and constructive?

903. How does your organization know that it is appropriately effective and constructive in preparing its staff for organizational aspirations?

904. Are complaint files maintained?

905. How does your organization know whether they are adhering to mission and achieving objectives?

906. Is there a risk that information provided by management may not always be reliable?

907. How does your organization know that its research programs are appropriately effective and constructive?

908. Do the acceptance procedures and specifications include the criteria for acceptance/rejection, define the process to be used, and specify the measuring and test equipment that is to be used?

909. Does the audit organization have experience in performing the required work for entities of your type and size?

910. How does your organization know that its staffing profile is optimally aligned with the capability requirements implicit (or explicit) in its Strategic Plan?

911. Does everyone know what they are supposed to be doing, how and why?

912. How does your organization know that its management of its ethical responsibilities is appropriately effective and constructive?

913. Will the evidence likely be sufficient and appropriate?

914. How does your organization know that its system for governing staff behaviour is appropriately effective and constructive?

915. Is your organizational structure a help or a hindrance to deployment?

3.6 Team Directory: Project Management

916. Contract requirements complied with?

917. Where should the information be distributed?

918. Days from the time the issue is identified?

919. Process decisions: how well was task order work performed?

920. Who will report Project Management project status to all stakeholders?

921. Who are the Team Members?

922. Decisions: is the most suitable form of contract being used?

923. Have you decided when to celebrate the Project Management projects completion date?

924. Who will write the meeting minutes and distribute?

925. Do purchase specifications and configurations match requirements?

926. Timing: when do the effects of communication take place?

927. Process decisions: are there any statutory or

regulatory issues relevant to the timely execution of work?

928. What are you going to deliver or accomplish?

929. Who will be the stakeholders on your next Project Management project?

930. Who is the Sponsor?

931. How will you accomplish and manage the objectives?

932. Why is the work necessary?

933. Does a Project Management project team directory list all resources assigned to the Project Management project?

934. What needs to be communicated?

3.7 Team Operating Agreement: Project Management

935. Do you solicit member feedback about meetings and what would make them better?

936. Seconds for members to respond?

937. Do you upload presentation materials in advance and test the technology?

938. Do you listen for voice tone and word choice to understand the meaning behind words?

939. Did you prepare participants for the next meeting?

940. How will your group handle planned absences?

941. Are there more than two native languages represented by your team?

942. Confidentiality: how will confidential information be handled?

943. Has the appropriate access to relevant data and analysis capability been granted?

944. Do you brief absent members after they view meeting notes or listen to a recording?

945. How do you want to be thought of and known within your organization?

946. Conflict resolution: how will disputes and other conflicts be mediated or resolved?

947. Did you determine the technology methods that best match the messages to be communicated?

948. Do you record meetings for the already stated unable to attend?

949. Communication protocols: how will the team communicate?

950. Do you prevent individuals from dominating the meeting?

951. Do you call or email participants to ensure understanding, follow-through and commitment to the meeting outcomes?

952. Do you post any action items, due dates, and responsibilities on the team website?

953. Do you use a parking lot for any items that are important and outside of the agenda?

954. What is the number of cases currently teamed?

3.8 Team Performance Assessment: Project Management

955. How much interpersonal friction is there in your team?

956. Delaying market entry: how long is too long?

957. What makes opportunities more or less obvious?

958. Do you give group members authority to make at least some important decisions?

959. What structural changes have you made or are you preparing to make?

960. Do friends perform better than acquaintances?

961. To what degree does the teams work approach provide opportunity for members to engage in fact-based problem solving?

962. To what degree do members understand and articulate the same purpose without relying on ambiguous abstractions?

963. To what degree is there a sense that only the team can succeed?

964. What is method variance?

965. To what degree will team members, individually and collectively, commit time to help themselves and

others learn and develop skills?

966. When a reviewer complains about method variance, what is the essence of the complaint?

967. Social categorization and intergroup behaviour: Does minimal intergroup discrimination make social identity more positive?

968. To what degree do members articulate the goals beyond the team membership?

969. Which situations call for a more extreme type of adaptiveness in which team members actually re-define roles?

970. How do you encourage members to learn from each other?

971. If you have received criticism from reviewers that your work suffered from method variance, what was the circumstance?

972. What are you doing specifically to develop the leaders around you?

973. To what degree are the teams goals and objectives clear, simple, and measurable?

974. To what degree will new and supplemental skills be introduced as the need is recognized?

3.9 Team Member Performance Assessment: Project Management

975. How are evaluation results utilized?

976. How do you use data to inform instruction and improve staff achievement?

977. How is the timing of assessments organized (e.g., pre/post-test, single point during training, multiple reassessment during training)?

978. Are assessment validation activities performed?

979. Does adaptive training work?

980. Are any governance changes sufficient to impact achievement?

981. Is it clear how goals will be accomplished?

982. Does the rater (supervisor) have to wait for the interim or final performance assessment review to tell an employee that the employees performance is unsatisfactory?

983. How does your team work together?

984. To what degree are the skill areas critical to team performance present?

985. To what degree are the goals realistic?

986. What happens if a team member disagrees with the Job Expectations?

987. How do you currently use the time that is available?

988. What is the role of the Reviewer?

989. How do you start collaborating?

990. To what degree does the teams purpose contain themes that are particularly meaningful and memorable?

991. How do you make use of research?

992. Is there reluctance to join a team?

3.10 Issue Log: Project Management

993. Who have you worked with in past, similar initiatives?

994. Which stakeholders are thought leaders, influences, or early adopters?

995. Are the stakeholders getting the information they need, are they consulted, are concerns addressed?

996. Are stakeholder roles recognized by your organization?

997. Do you feel more overwhelmed by stakeholders?

998. Can you think of other people who might have concerns or interests?

999. Who is the stakeholder?

1000. What steps can you take for positive relationships?

1001. How were past initiatives successful?

1002. What is the status of the issue?

1003. What are the stakeholders interrelationships?

1004. What is the impact on the risks?

1005. Is there an important stakeholder who is

actively opposed and will not receive messages?

1006. Are they needed?

1007. Who do you turn to if you have questions?

1008. Who is the issue assigned to?

1009. How do you manage human resources?

1010. What are the typical contents?

1011. What approaches do you use?

4.0 Monitoring and Controlling Process Group: Project Management

1012. Did the Project Management project team have enough people to execute the Project Management project plan?

1013. What are the goals of the program?

1014. If action is called for, what form should it take?

1015. Is progress on outcomes due to your program?

1016. How were collaborations developed, and how are they sustained?

1017. Mitigate. what will you do to minimize the impact should a risk event occur?

1018. Accuracy: what design will lead to accurate information?

1019. Who are the Project Management project stakeholders?

1020. What is the timeline?

1021. Is the program in place as intended?

1022. What business situation is being addressed?

1023. How was the program set-up initiated?

1024. Do the partners have sufficient financial capacity to keep up the benefits produced by the programme?

1025. Are the services being delivered?

1026. Is the program making progress in helping to achieve the set results?

1027. Is there undesirable impact on staff or resources?

4.1 Project Performance Report: Project Management

1028. To what degree are the demands of the task compatible with and converge with the mission and functions of the formal organization?

1029. How is the data used?

1030. To what degree are the demands of the task compatible with and converge with the relationships of the informal organization?

1031. To what degree can all members engage in open and interactive considerations?

1032. To what degree can the team measure progress against specific goals?

1033. To what degree do team members articulate the teams work approach?

1034. To what degree do the relationships of the informal organization motivate taskrelevant behavior and facilitate task completion?

1035. Next Steps?

1036. How can Project Management project sustainability be maintained?

1037. To what degree do all members feel responsible for all agreed-upon measures?

1038. To what degree are the tasks requirements reflected in the flow and storage of information?

1039. To what degree are sub-teams possible or necessary?

1040. To what degree does the information network provide individuals with the information they require?

1041. To what degree do individual skills and abilities match task demands?

1042. To what degree is the information network consistent with the structure of the formal organization?

1043. To what degree will each member have the opportunity to advance his or her professional skills in all three of the above categories while contributing to the accomplishment of the teams purpose and goals?

1044. What is the degree to which rules govern information exchange between individuals within your organization?

4.2 Variance Analysis: Project Management

1045. Is the anticipated (firm and potential) business base Project Management projected in a rational, consistent manner?

1046. Favorable or unfavorable variance?

1047. How does your organization allocate the cost of shared expenses and services?

1048. Does the contractor use objective results, design reviews and tests to trace schedule performance?

1049. Are overhead cost budgets established for each department which has authority to incur overhead costs?

1050. Budget versus actual. how does the monthly budget compare to actual experience?

1051. How do you evaluate the impact of schedule changes, work around, et?

1052. Are indirect costs accumulated for comparison with the corresponding budgets?

1053. Are control accounts opened and closed based on the start and completion of work contained therein?

1054. Do you identify potential or actual budget-based and time-based schedule variances?

1055. Who is generally responsible for monitoring and taking action on variances?

1056. Are all budgets assigned to control accounts?

1057. Are work packages assigned to performing organizations?

1058. How does the use of a single conversion element (rather than the traditional labor and overhead elements) affect standard costing?

1059. Why are standard cost systems used?

1060. Are your organizations and items of cost assigned to each pool identified?

4.3 Earned Value Status: Project Management

1061. Verification is a process of ensuring that the developed system satisfies the stakeholders agreements and specifications; Are you building the product right? What do you verify?

1062. Where is evidence-based earned value in your organization reported?

1063. Validation is a process of ensuring that the developed system will actually achieve the stakeholders desired outcomes; Are you building the right product? What do you validate?

1064. When is it going to finish?

1065. Earned value can be used in almost any Project Management project situation and in almost any Project Management project environment. it may be used on large Project Management projects, medium sized Project Management projects, tiny Project Management projects (in cut-down form), complex and simple Project Management projects and in any market sector. some people, of course, know all about earned value, they have used it for years - but perhaps not as effectively as they could have?

1066. How does this compare with other Project Management projects?

1067. If earned value management (EVM) is so good in

determining the true status of a Project Management project and Project Management project its completion, why is it that hardly any one uses it in information systems related Project Management projects?

1068. What is the unit of forecast value?

1069. Are you hitting your Project Management projects targets?

1070. Where are your problem areas?

1071. How much is it going to cost by the finish?

4.4 Risk Audit: Project Management

1072. Is the auditor truly independent?

1073. If applicable; which route/packaging option do you choose for transport of hazmat material?

1074. Do you have position descriptions for all office bearers/staff?

1075. Has an event time line been developed?

1076. Are procedures in place to ensure the security of staff and information and compliance with privacy legislation if applicable?

1077. What expertise do auditors need to generate effective business-level risk assessments, and to what extent do auditors currently possess the already stated attributes?

1078. Do you have a mechanism for managing change?

1079. What compliance systems do you have in place to address quality, errors, and outcomes?

1080. Do you meet all obligations relating to funds secured from grants, loans and sponsors?

1081. Does your organization communicate regularly and effectively with its members?

1082. Which assets are important?

1083. Is an annual audit required and conducted of your financial records?

1084. Are Project Management project requirements stable?

1085. What risk does not having unique identification present?

1086. Do you have a procedure for dealing with complaints?

1087. What events or circumstances could affect the achievement of your objectives?

1088. Do you have a realistic budget and do you present regular financial reports that identify how you are going against that budget?

1089. Have all possible risks/hazards been identified (including injury to staff, damage to equipment, impact on others in the community)?

1090. What can you do to manage outcomes?

1091. What impact does prior experience have on decisions made during the risk-assessment process?

4.5 Contractor Status Report: Project Management

1092. How is risk transferred?

1093. Who can list a Project Management project as organization experience, your organization or a previous employee of your organization?

1094. If applicable; describe your standard schedule for new software version releases. Are new software version releases included in the standard maintenance plan?

1095. What was the final actual cost?

1096. What is the average response time for answering a support call?

1097. How long have you been using the services?

1098. Describe how often regular updates are made to the proposed solution. Are corresponding regular updates included in the standard maintenance plan?

1099. Are there contractual transfer concerns?

1100. What was the overall budget or estimated cost?

1101. How does the proposed individual meet each requirement?

1102. What was the actual budget or estimated cost

for your organizations services?

1103. What was the budget or estimated cost for your organizations services?

1104. What are the minimum and optimal bandwidth requirements for the proposed soluiton?

1105. What process manages the contracts?

4.6 Formal Acceptance: Project Management

1106. Was the client satisfied with the Project Management project results?

1107. Does it do what client said it would?

1108. Was business value realized?

1109. Was the Project Management project managed well?

1110. Was the Project Management project goal achieved?

1111. What was done right?

1112. Do you buy pre-configured systems or build your own configuration?

1113. How does your team plan to obtain formal acceptance on your Project Management project?

1114. What function(s) does it fill or meet?

1115. Do you perform formal acceptance or burn-in tests?

1116. Was the Project Management project work done on time, within budget, and according to specification?

1117. How well did the team follow the methodology?

1118. Who would use it?

1119. Was the sponsor/customer satisfied?

1120. Is formal acceptance of the Project Management project product documented and distributed?

1121. Have all comments been addressed?

1122. What can you do better next time?

1123. What lessons were learned about your Project Management project management methodology?

1124. Who supplies data?

1125. Did the Project Management project manager and team act in a professional and ethical manner?

5.0 Closing Process Group: Project Management

1126. How well did the chosen processes fit the needs of the Project Management project?

1127. Were cost budgets met?

1128. What is an Encumbrance?

1129. Did you do things well?

1130. Is the Project Management project funded?

1131. Did the delivered product meet the specified requirements and goals of the Project Management project?

1132. Just how important is your work to the overall success of the Project Management project?

1133. How will you know you did it?

1134. Were risks identified and mitigated?

1135. What was learned?

1136. Did the Project Management project management methodology work?

1137. Can the lesson learned be replicated?

1138. How will you do it?

1139. How well defined and documented were the Project Management project management processes you chose to use?

5.1 Procurement Audit: Project Management

1140. Are all mutilated and voided checks retained for proper accounting of pre-numbered checks?

1141. Do staff involved in the various stages of the process have the appropriate skills and training to perform duties effectively?

1142. Are there performance targets on value for money obtained and cost savings?

1143. Are travel expenditures monitored to determine that they are in line with other employees and reasonable for the area of travel?

1144. Were results of the award procedures published?

1145. Does the procurement function/unit have the ability to secure best performance from contractors?

1146. Does an appropriately qualified official check the quality of performance against the contract terms?

1147. Is a cash flow chart prepared and used in determining the timing and term of investments?

1148. Did the additional works introduce minor or non-substantial changes to performance, as described in the contract documents?

1149. Are all initial purchase contracts made by the purchasing organization?

1150. If an order is divided among several vendors, is the explanation for that procedure documented?

1151. Did the chosen procedure ensure fair competition and transparency?

1152. Does the procurement function/unit have the ability to apply electronic procurement?

1153. Are unusual uses of organization funds investigated?

1154. Is the purchasing department facility laid out to facilitate interviews with salespersons?

1155. Do appropriate controls ensure that procurement decisions are not biased by conflicts of interest or corruption?

1156. Are purchasing actions processed on a timely basis?

1157. Is the appropriate procurement approach being chosen (considering for example the possibility of contracting out work or procuring low value items through a specific low cost procuring system)?

1158. Is the strategy implemented across the entire organization?

1159. Are the users needs clearly and invariably defined and has the expected outcome or mission been clearly identified and communicated in measurable terms?

5.2 Contract Close-Out: Project Management

1160. Change in attitude or behavior?

1161. How is the contracting office notified of the automatic contract close-out?

1162. Has each contract been audited to verify acceptance and delivery?

1163. What happens to the recipient of services?

1164. Have all contract records been included in the Project Management project archives?

1165. How/when used ?

1166. What is capture management?

1167. Parties: Authorized?

1168. Was the contract complete without requiring numerous changes and revisions?

1169. Are the signers the authorized officials?

1170. Have all acceptance criteria been met prior to final payment to contractors?

1171. How does it work?

1172. Change in knowledge?

1173. Was the contract sufficiently clear so as not to result in numerous disputes and misunderstandings?

1174. Parties: who is involved?

1175. Change in circumstances?

1176. Have all contracts been closed?

1177. Was the contract type appropriate?

1178. Have all contracts been completed?

1179. Why Outsource?

5.3 Project or Phase Close-Out: Project Management

1180. Who controlled the resources for the Project Management project?

1181. What information did each stakeholder need to contribute to the Project Management projects success?

1182. What is the information level of detail required for each stakeholder?

1183. What could be done to improve the process?

1184. What are the mandatory communication needs for each stakeholder?

1185. What were the actual outcomes?

1186. Does the lesson educate others to improve performance?

1187. Were the outcomes different from the already stated planned?

1188. Is the lesson based on actual Project Management project experience rather than on independent research?

1189. Who controlled key decisions that were made?

1190. What is this stakeholder expecting?

1191. Did the delivered product meet the specified requirements and goals of the Project Management project?

1192. Which changes might a stakeholder be required to make as a result of the Project Management project?

1193. What process was planned for managing issues/ risks?

1194. In addition to assessing whether the Project Management project was successful, it is equally critical to analyze why it was or was not fully successful. Are you including this?

1195. What are they?

1196. How often did each stakeholder need an update?

1197. What hierarchical authority does the stakeholder have in your organization?

5.4 Lessons Learned: Project Management

1198. Was the purpose of the Project Management project, the end products and success criteria clearly defined and agreed at the start?

1199. How effectively and consistently was sponsorship for the Project Management project conveyed?

1200. How well does the product or service the Project Management project produced meet the defined Project Management project requirements?

1201. How well defined were the acceptance criteria for Project Management project deliverables?

1202. What regulatory regime controlled how your organization head and program manager directed your organization and Project Management project?

1203. How clearly defined were the objectives for this Project Management project?

1204. What worked well or did not work well, either for this Project Management project or for the Project Management project team?

1205. Did the Project Management project management methodology work?

1206. Overall, how effective was the performance of

the Project Management project Manager?

1207. Was any formal risk assessment carried out at the start of the Project Management project, and was this followed up during the Project Management project?

1208. How well do you feel the executives supported this Project Management project?

1209. How much flexibility is there in the funding (e.g., what authorities does the program manager have to change to the specifics of the funding within the overall funding ceiling)?

1210. How effective was each Project Management project Team member in fulfilling his/her role?

1211. How accurately and timely was the Risk Management Log updated or reviewed?

1212. Did the Project Management project improve the team members reputations, skills, personal development?

1213. How timely were Progress Reports provided to the Project Management project Manager by Team Members?

1214. Was the necessary hardware, software, accommodation etc available?

1215. How satisfied are you with your involvement in the development and/or review of the Project Management project Scope during Project Management project Initiation and Planning?

1216. Overall, how effective were the efforts to prepare you and your organization for the impact of the product/service of the Project Management project?

1217. How comprehensive was integration testing?

Index

286

prevent   19-21, 24, 62, 150, 161, 167, 210, 227, 242
previous   29, 125, 259
previously   149, 233
primarily   103, 204
primary   57, 76, 127
principles   42, 61, 119, 128
printing   8
priorities   46
prioritize   44-45
priority 43, 48, 171, 224
Privacy 22, 30, 257
probable   215
probably   178
problem   17, 25-26, 28-29, 35-36, 38, 53, 103, 152, 228, 235, 243, 256
problems   17-20, 22, 47, 78, 88, 111, 154, 196, 198, 208
procedure   100, 110, 123, 134, 258, 266
procedures   11, 22, 30, 57, 60, 71, 81, 83-84, 86, 88-89, 92-93, 119, 132, 135, 150, 177, 184, 198, 218, 224, 231, 234, 237, 257, 265
proceeding   182, 186
process   1-7, 11, 25, 29-30, 32, 37-39, 41-44, 48-50, 52-64, 66, 69, 71, 75, 81-83, 85-92, 103, 113, 130, 139-140, 146-147, 152-154, 156, 158-161, 166, 168, 177, 180-182, 195, 198-199, 209, 212, 214, 219, 221, 226-227, 235, 237, 239, 249, 255, 258, 260, 263, 265, 270-271
processed   266
processes   31, 42, 52, 54-56, 58, 60-63, 84-86, 93, 104, 126, 129, 150, 159-160, 194, 198, 208, 223, 227, 233, 263-264
procure   59
procuring   226, 266
produce   177, 188, 229
produced   50, 60-61, 158, 250, 272
producing   156
product   1, 11, 45-46, 58, 66, 68, 70-72, 76, 80, 97, 115, 120, 125-127, 130, 152, 160, 173-174, 192-193, 197, 209, 226, 229, 233, 255, 262-263, 271-272, 274
production   90, 131, 134
productive   131
products   1, 59, 115, 121, 147, 156, 167, 181, 213, 228, 232, 272
profile 47, 210, 237
profits 193

special 45, 54, 91, 224
specialist   106
specific   9, 25, 29, 31, 35, 60, 72, 98, 110, 114, 135, 152,
159, 170-171, 174, 177, 184, 195, 202-204, 213, 220, 227-228, 233,
251, 266
specifics   273
specified   164, 217, 263, 271
specify 237
specifying   115
spending   114
sphere 72
sponsor   22, 148, 158, 222, 226, 240, 262
sponsored   37
sponsors   24, 199, 218, 224, 257
spread 98
sprint   107
stability 42
stable   152, 208, 258
staffed 33
staffing 73, 93, 132, 148, 160, 237
staffs   126
stages 66, 151, 265
standard   7, 83, 85, 93, 177, 180, 196, 204, 254, 259
standards   1, 11-12, 80, 83-84, 88, 90-91, 93, 119, 160-161,
165, 195-197, 199, 233, 236
started 9, 81, 112
starting 12
starts   88
start-up   145
start-ups   45
stated 44, 55, 196, 242, 257, 270
statement   3, 12, 150, 158-159, 188, 193
statements   13, 27, 35-36, 40, 51, 53, 64, 79, 94, 136
status 5-6, 25, 42, 47, 49, 117, 130, 132, 140, 151, 165, 168, 201,
204, 228, 239, 247, 255-256, 259
statutory   239
Steering   20
storage   198, 252
strategic   54, 86, 93, 107, 151, 195, 204, 210, 237
strategies   204, 213, 218, 234
strategy   23, 70, 76, 101, 104-105, 108, 121-122, 124, 129,
146-147, 151, 188, 211, 218, 234, 266
strengths   54, 102, 120, 144

strong 114
Strongly   12, 17, 28, 41, 52, 65, 80, 95
structural   243
structure   3-4, 42, 51, 53, 74, 96, 103, 107, 136, 159, 162-163, 178, 184, 238, 252
structured   167
structures   126, 147, 165
subdivide   165
subdivided   201
subject9-10, 37, 112, 153
submit 11
submitted   11, 233
submitting   196
sub-teams   252
subtotals   188
succeed   55, 105, 243
success   22-23, 30, 34, 43, 50, 70, 86, 105, 111, 125-126, 128, 130, 139, 141-142, 147, 150, 167, 175, 186, 214, 226, 229, 263, 270, 272
successful   18, 26, 42, 54, 65, 69-70, 85, 90, 103, 128, 146, 228, 247, 271
successor   107
suffered   244
sufficient   25, 31, 54, 61, 106, 147, 164, 236-237, 245, 250
suggested   88, 232-233
suggests   95
suitable   48, 213, 239
supervisor   245
suppliers   32, 186
supplies   167, 262
supply 61, 116, 119
support   7, 19, 68, 73-75, 77, 84-85, 88, 97, 107, 124, 127, 136, 141, 144, 177, 195, 203, 214, 224, 234, 236, 259
supported   38, 53, 147, 212, 273
supporting   60, 218
supports   115
supposed   237
surface   88
surprise145
SUSTAIN   2, 95
sustained   188, 249
sustaining   90
symptom   17

314

316

CPSIA information can be obtained
at www.ICGtesting.com
Printed in the USA
BVHW080803220419
546159BV00025B/1679/P